M000188236

THE SEPTUAGINT

Other books in the Understanding the Bible and its World series:

THE SEPTUAGINT

JENNIFER M. DINES

Edited by
Michael A. Knibb

T & T CLARK
A Continuum imprint
LONDON • NEW YORK

T&T CLARK LTD
A Continuum imprint

The Tower Building, 11 York Road,   15 East 26th Street, Suite 1703,
London SE1 7NX   New York, NY 10010

www.tandtclark.com

Copyright © 2004 Jennifer M. Dines

All rights reserved. No part of this publication may be reproduced or
transmitted in any form or by any means, electronic or mechanical, including
photocopying, recording or any information storage or retrieval system,
without permission in writing from the publishers.

ISBN 0 567 08464 7

British Library Cataloguing-in-Publication Data
A catalogue record for this book is available from the British Library

Typeset by Tradespools, Frome, Somerset
Printed on acid-free paper in Great Britain by The Bath Press, Bath

Contents

Preface

The Septuagint – the Greek Bible – represents the first known attempt to translate the Hebrew Scriptures into an Indo-European language. It stands at the very beginning of the history of the diffusion and interpretation of the Bible in translation. It consists of Greek versions of all the books of the Hebrew Scriptures (the Jewish 'Tanakh' and the Christian 'Old Testament') and a number of Greek apocryphal (or deuterocanonical) works: the additions to Esther, Jeremiah and Daniel, 1–4 Maccabees, Tobit, Judith, I Esdras, Wisdom, Sirach and the Psalms of Solomon. These apocryphal and pseudepigraphical books, although Jewish in origin, owe their survival to their preservation in Christian biblical manuscripts, that is, to their inclusion in 'the Septuagint' and they are integral to its study.

The Greek Bible is important for our understanding of both Greek-speaking Hellenistic Judaism (almost all the translations were made between the third and first centuries BCE) and emerging Christianity. It provides our earliest evidence for the way in which the Hebrew Scriptures were understood by non-Hebrew-speaking readers, both Jewish and Christian. It also contributes to our knowledge of Koine Greek. All these aspects will be examined in the context of modern scholarly research, although the discussions, given limitations of space, are necessarily little more than pointers to further study.

Chapter 1 supplies some basic information, the minimum necessary for making sense of contemporary scholarly debates. It also outlines the character of individual books, and their

ix

particular interest for Septuagint studies. Chapters 2 and 3 discuss evidence for and theories about historical origins, and the questions and issues involved, while Chapter 4 traces changing attitudes towards the Greek Scriptures in Jewish and Christian authors until the fifth century CE. Chapters 5 and 6 address linguistic, translational and text-critical issues essential to understanding how the Septuagint may be understood both as a collection of Hellenistic texts and in relation to its parent-text, the Hebrew Bible. Finally, Chapter 7 examines some significant contributions of the Septuagint to early biblical interpretation and returns to the importance of the Septuagint for knowledge of the period which saw the emergence of both Hellenistic Judaism and early Christianity.

The seeds of this book were sown several years ago in postgraduate classes and seminars at Heythrop College, University of London. That the seeds germinated and grew owes much to the interest and encouragement of Dr Marie Isaacs (then Head of the Biblical Studies Department), and of my other friends and colleagues in the Department: Joe Mulrooney, Tom Deidun, Ann Jeffers and Bridget Gilfillan Upton. To them, to Dr Robert Murray (who first encouraged my interest in the Greek Bible) and to my various 'Septua-gintal' students, my warmest thanks and appreciation are offered. More recently, my conviction of the necessity for grounding the Septuagint in the world of its Hellenistic origins, has been nourished by exchanges with members of the 'Greek Bible in the Graeco-Roman World' project (sponsored by the Arts and Humanities Research Board Parkes Centre), especially Professor Tessa Rajak, Dr Sarah Pearce and Dr James Aitken.

My thanks are also due to members of the Hebrew, Jewish and Early Christian Studies Seminar at Cambridge for their helpful responses to a 'work in progress' paper in May 2002 which became part of Chapter 3. I am particularly grateful to Dr James Aitken for reading and commenting on a draft version of the whole typescript, and to Professor Michael Knibb for his patient and respectful editorial guidance at an earlier stage when the book was destined for the 'Guides to the Apocrypha and Pseudepigrapha' series.

Unavoidable delays in completing this book have had one positive effect: they have enabled me to take advantage of the English edition of Natalio Fernández Marcos's *Septuagint in Context,* and of Karen Jobes's and Moisés Silva's *Invitation to the Septuagint.* Both will be frequently cited. I have not, however, been able to use Folker Siegert's new German introduction.

Jennifer M. Dines
Cambridge, May 2003

for my parents

Reggie Dines
and
Jessica Mary Constance Bagley

in loving and grateful memory

Abbreviations

AB	Anchor Bible
ABD	*The Anchor Bible Dictionary*, ed. D. N. Freedman *et al.* (1992)
Ant.	*Antiquities of the Jews*
ANRW	*Aufstieg und Niedergang der Römischer Welt*
BA	La Bible d'Alexandrie
BIOSCS	*Bulletin of the International Organization for Septuagint and Cognate Studies*
BJGS	*Bulletin of Judaeo-Greek Studies*
BZAW	*Beihefte zur Zeitschrift für die alttestamentliche Wissenschaft*
CATSS	Computer Assisted Tools for the Study of the Septuagint
CNRS	Centre National de la Recherche Scientifique
CSIC	Consejo Superior de Investigationes Científicas
DBI	*The Dictionary of Biblical Interpretation*, ed. J. Hayes (1999)
DJD	Discoveries in the Judaean Desert
Ep. Arist.	*The Letter of Aristeas to Philocrates*
HE	*Historia Ecclesiae*
HeyJ	*The Heythrop Journal*
HUCA	*Hebrew Union College Annual*
IOSCS	International Organization for Septuagint and Cognate Studies
JJS	*Journal of Jewish Studies*
JNSL	*Journal of North-West Semitic Literature*

JSJ	*Journal for the Study of Judaism in the Persian, Hellenistic and Roman Period*
JSOT	*Journal for the Study of the Old Testament*
JTS	*Journal of Theological Studies*
LCL	Loeb Classical Library
LXX	The Septuagint
MSU	Mitteilungen des Septuaginta-Unternehmens
MT	Masoretic Text
NETS	A New English Translation of the Septuagint
NRSV	New Revised Standard Version
NT	The New Testament
OG	Old Greek
OL	Old Latin
OT	The Old Testament
OTS	*Oudtestamentische Studiën*
PAAJR	*Proceedings of the American Academy for Jewish Research*
PE	*Praeparatio Evangelica*
PIBA	*Proceedings of the Irish Biblical Association*
REB	Revised English Bible
RTL	*Revue théologique de Louvain*
RTP	*Revue de théologie et de philosophie*
SBL	Society of Biblical Literature
SC	Sources chrétiennes
TU	Texte und Untersuchungen
VC	*Vigiliae christianae*
VL	Vetus Latina
VT	*Vetus Testamentum*
VTSup	*Vetus Testamentum* Supplements

Resources

To study 'the Septuagint' is to study entire Bibles! Here, space allows only a few items to be suggested under each heading. More detailed information is available in the General introductions (below) and in the 'Further reading' sections at the end of each chapter. A good way to follow current developments is to consult the annual *Bulletin of the International Organization for Septuagint and Cognate Studies* (*BIOSCS*), and the Organization's Congress Volumes (some are listed in the general Bibliography).

(1) General introductions

For the beginner, the most up-to-date, accessible and useful work is currently Jobes and Silva (2000). For in-depth treatment of many important issues, Fernández Marcos (2000) is essential reading; as the English version unfortunately contains many errors, the revised Spanish edition (Fernández Marcos 1998) should also be consulted, if possible. Both build on earlier treatments, especially those of Swete (1914), Jellicoe (1968) and Harl, Dorival and Munnich (1988; this is particularly valuable for its succinct summary discussions).

(2) The text in Greek

Rahlfs (1935) prints the entire Septuagint together with brief critical apparatus and is the most practical edition for reading and general study. For detailed textual work, editions of the

Göttingen Septuagint (1931–) should be used or, where these are not yet published, the editions of Brooke, McLean and Thackeray (1906–40).

(3) Translations

a. *In English.* Brenton (1851; first published, without the Apocrypha, in 1844), although out-dated and often inaccurate, is the only complete version (including Apocrypha) easily available. The first volume in the New English Translation of the Septuagint (NETS) series (Psalms) has now been published (Pietersma 2000a); the remaining volumes are due to appear in the near future.
b. *In French.* La Bible d'Alexandrie (BA, 1986–) is an ongoing book-by-book series. Dogniez and Harl (2001) provide a one-volume edition of the BA Pentateuch.

(4) Bibliographies

Brock, Fritsch and Jellicoe (1973) and Dogniez (1995) provide detailed classified bibliographies up to 1993.

(5) Dictionaries

There is no large-scale lexicon of the Septuagint. Dictionaries of the New Testament (NT), and classical Greek lexicons give some coverage. Lust, Eynikel and Hauspie (1992) is short, but specifically on the Septuagint. Muraoka (2002a) covers the Pentateuch and the Minor Prophets.

(6) Concordances

Hatch and Redpath (1897–1906) is still an essential research tool. Muraoka (1998) provides a reverse index.

(7) Grammars

Thackeray (1909), Conybeare and Stock (1905) and Taylor (1994) are specifically on the Septuagint. Lexical and grammatical help can also be found in grammars of the NT and in various computer software programs, e.g. 'BibleWorks for Windows' (Big Fork, Montana: Hermeneutika Bible Research Software™, 1999). For Mac users, the 'Accordance' program (Oaktree Software) is available (see Jobes and Silva 2000: 323 for details).

(8) Information Technology

Computer software packages and websites are proliferating, and provide ever-increasing facilities for study and research. Specifically designed for textual work on the Septuagint is the CATSS project (Computer Assisted Tools for the Study of the Septuagint. See Jobes and Silva 2000: 316–17; Tov 1997: 90–1; McLay 1999: 44–6). The CATSS web address is http://ccat.sas.upenn.edu (see *BIOSCS* 31(1998): 53, n. 1). Some useful websites are surveyed by Knobloch (1998: 47–59; 2000: 36–8). New websites are, of course, being developed all the time (see e.g. http://www.rdg.ac.uk/lxx, for the 'Greek Bible in the Graeco-Roman World' project already mentioned, to give just one recent example).

CHAPTER 1

What is 'the Septuagint'?

Writing in the first century CE, the Jewish author Philo of Alexandria described the Mosaic Scriptures in Greek as a 'good gift' from Jews to the Greek-speaking world (*De Vita Mosis* 2.41). In our own time, the Septuagint (LXX), the first sustained translation of Semitic sacred texts into an Indo-European language, has been called a 'phenomenon' (Brock 1972: 11). Both linguistically and culturally, the LXX is a remarkable achievement of Hellenistic Judaism, with subsequent impact on early Christianity, and is of major importance for biblical and other studies today. Before we explore some of these areas, it will be helpful to consider what is meant by 'the Septuagint' in order to avoid confusion in subsequent discussions.

Terminology

The term 'Septuagint' is surprisingly slippery. It is derived from Latin *septuaginta*, meaning 'seventy'; the standard abbreviation, LXX, is the numerical Latin equivalent. As a title, *Septuaginta* is abbreviated from *interpretatio septuaginta virorum* ('the translation by the seventy men') or similar expressions. The Greek equivalent, found in manuscripts from the fourth century CE onwards, is *kata tous hebdomēkonta*, 'according to the seventy', or similar. It is a kind of shorthand, reflecting early legends about seventy or, more properly, seventy-two original translators of the Pentateuch. The stories

1

are preserved in a Hellenistic Jewish work, the pseudepigraphical *Letter of Aristeas to Philocrates* (*Ep. Arist.*) and in other
early sources, both Jewish and Christian (see Chapter 2).
Although the traditions do occur in rabbinic Jewish sources
(see Orlinsky 1989: 537–8; Veltri 1994), the great majority of
references to 'the Seventy' occur in Christian writers. The
earliest are in Irenaeus (*Against Heresies* 3.21.3) and Tertullian
(*Apology* 18) in the second century CE. In the fourth century,
Augustine (*City of God* 18.42) quotes 'Septuaginta' as the usual
term (Swete 1914: 9–10).

Scope of the term in antiquity

When the earliest Jewish sources refer to the Greek translations, they apparently mean only the five books attributed to
Moses (Tov 1988: 163). Christian authors, however, from
Justin in the second century CE and onwards, refer to the work
of the Seventy as covering any or all of the books of the Bible
in Greek which were accepted by Christians. The earliest
comprehensive manuscripts, from the fourth and fifth
centuries CE, indicate that 'the Septuagint' embraces all the
books of the Hebrew canon. In addition, each manuscript has
its own selection of apocryphal and pseudepigraphical works,
variously inserted among the canonical books, showing that
different Christian communities still had different preferences. So 'Septuagint' may cover different contents when it
refers to particular manuscripts.

*Scope of the term in contemporary usage: 'Septuagint' and/or 'Old
Greek'?*

Nowadays, 'Septuagint' is used in a variety of ways. (1) It
sometimes refers to the Greek version of a particular book
(e.g. 'Septuagint Psalms', 'the Septuagint of Jonah') as distinct
from either the corresponding Hebrew book or, in some cases,
alternative ancient Greek versions. In the case of Daniel, for
instance, the 'Septuagint' version has to be distinguished from
that of 'Theodotion', which was in more common use. (2) In
some books, particularly parts of Judges and Samuel-Kings, it is
clear that our oldest manuscripts have transmitted revised

forms of the original translation. 'Septuagint' here is sometimes used loosely for the whole manuscript tradition, sometimes more correctly for the original material only. (3)
Sometimes it is used very broadly, as in 'Septuagint studies',
or 'printed editions of the Septuagint' (individual authors and
editors will make it clear whether or not the apocryphal and
pseudepigraphical books are included).

Some scholars prefer to use the term 'Old Greek (OG)'
instead of 'Septuagint' for the earliest stage that can be
reconstructed for any book. 'Septuagint' or 'LXX' is then kept
for the subsequent stages of textual transmission. Sometimes
the term 'Proto-Septuagint' is used for the hypothetical
reconstructed originals, but more often it is the modern
critical editions that are presented as 'the Septuagint' (e.g.
Rahlfs 1935 or the Göttingen Septuagint). Some scholars have
tried to keep distinctions clear (see e.g. Peters 1992: 1093–4;
Tov 1997: xiii, 237), but not all are so punctilious.

There is, in fact, no agreed code of practice, and
terminology must be checked against the usage of any given
scholar (although they may not always be consistent). Greenspoon's protest against an unnecessary proliferation of
definitions is timely (1987: 21–9). It is tempting to settle, as
he does, for a simple division between 'OG' for the earliest
stratum, and 'LXX' for the rest. But, as will become clear,
recovering this earliest stratum is problematic. In this book,
'LXX' will be used as the all-embracing term; its scope will be
specified where necessary.

Primary sources: manuscripts and editions

Most LXX users today rely on the printed critical editions. But
these are the outcome of collating vast numbers of manuscripts. As will be seen in Chapter 5, the history of the LXX's
early transmission has made it extremely difficult to recover
the original form of the text; indeed in some places it may
have been irretrievably lost. The major problems began in the
late-third century CE, in the wake of Origen's work (see
Chapter 5, p. 102. This means that any pre-Origenic

manuscripts, however fragmentary, are of great importance, especially when they come from a Jewish milieu. But because revision of the LXX began at least as far back as the first century BCE, even pre-Origenic material has to be examined with great care (the Washington Papyrus of the Minor Prophets from the third century CE, for example, has been partially adjusted to the standard Hebrew). The earliest evidence is Jewish, and comes from both Palestine and Egypt. This will be surveyed, very briefly, before the early Christian witnesses are considered.

The earliest Jewish manuscripts

(1) From the Judaean desert. So far, the earliest Greek biblical texts that we possess have been found among the Dead Sea Scrolls. They consist of fragments of Deuteronomy (4Q122, Deut. 11.4), Leviticus (4Q119, Lev. 26.2–16), Exodus (7Q1, Exod. 28.4–7) and *The Letter of Jeremiah* (7Q2), all dated to the second century BCE. Some of these already show signs of revision. It appears to have been of two kinds. Some alterations are intended, apparently, to improve the Greek style (e.g. 7Q2), while others apparently aim to bring the Greek into conformity with a Hebrew text resembling the later Masoretic Text (MT, e.g. 7Q1).

Further fragments of the Pentateuch date from the first century BCE or CE (e.g. 4Q120, Lev. 2–5; 4Q121, Num. 3.30–4.14; the latter shows signs of literary revision). From the late-first century BCE comes a fragmentary, but very important, scroll of the Minor Prophets (8ḤvXIIgr) which has been lightly but idiosyncratically revised against the emerging 'standard' Hebrew; it forms part of what has come to be called the *kaige* revision (see below, Chapter 5, pp. 81–4). Further fragments include parts of other prophetical and historical books.

The discovery among the Dead Sea Scrolls of substantial fragments of the LXX, even in a revised form, is some indication of the early spread of the translations and of their use by at least some Greek-speaking Palestinian Jews. It is particularly striking that the Minor Prophets scroll was found in a cave associated with the doomed revolt against the Romans in 132–35 CE of the Jewish leader, Simon Bar Kokhba. That Greek, as well as Hebrew and Aramaic, was a medium of communication even for ultra-nationalist Jews is reinforced by the discovery of despatches written in Greek by Bar Kokhba himself (Porter 2000a: 58–9; Yadin *et al.* 2002: 49–63).

(2) From Egypt. Important early papyrus witnesses to the LXX, in the geographical area where much of the translating is thought to have taken place, include substantial amounts of Deuteronomy (963, 957, 847, 848; the numbers assigned to the papyri are based on the list published by Rahlfs 1914). There are also small portions of Job (P.Oxyrh.3522) and Genesis (942). These are all datable to the second or first century BCE or the first century CE. They thus cover the same period as the Judaean finds (Kenyon 1975: 31). Material of this age is certainly Jewish. In addition to their textual importance (similar revisional touches are found as in the Qumran fragments), some papyri are significant for cultural reasons. Papyrus 957, for instance, which preserves about twenty verses of Deuteronomy 23–8, was found, together with other literary fragments (including parts of the *Iliad*) as mummy cartonnage. This raises interesting questions about the circulation and preservation of biblical texts at that time (the papyrus is currently dated to the second century BCE). How did a carefully written biblical scroll end up in this situation (in a later period an antiquated sacred writing would have been stored in a special room called a genizah)? Do we have evidence here of non-Jewish access to Jewish Scriptures? Or proof that Jews could be at home with classical Greek literature? There is not enough evidence to make any answers certain; the questions are, however, important (see further Roberts 1936: 11–32).

Once we reach the end of the first century CE, Greek biblical papyri are more likely to be of Christian origin (see below, Chapters 4 and 5). Some fragments, however, containing portions of Genesis (905, 907) and Psalms (2110) and dated to the second to fourth centuries CE, may be Jewish. If this were certain, it would be valuable evidence for continued Jewish use of the LXX (research into this is being carried out, for example, by R.A. Kraft). Interesting, too, is the fact that at least two of these papyri are in codex form, while a late-third-century fragment of Genesis 2–3 (907) is not only in codex form but written on parchment, not papyrus (Bogaert 1985: 199). These and other considerations bring into question the common assumption that use of the codex was an exclusively Christian development.

The earliest Christian manuscripts

Late-first-and even second-century CE papyri could be either Christian or Jewish and identifying them as one or the other can be problematic. Furthermore, the dating of papyri is not always certain. From the third century CE onwards, however, Greek biblical texts are most likely to be Christian. One of the most important pre-Origenic papyri, 967, from the late-second or early-third century CE, is a codex containing parts of Ezekiel, Esther and, very exceptionally, the LXX form of Daniel.

These and other remains, on parchment as well as papyrus, and in both scroll and codex form, antedate the first extant complete Bibles which date only from the fourth and fifth centuries. They help to fill in some of the gaps in our knowledge before Christianity became established as the official religion of the Empire in the mid-fourth century.

The first Bibles (the major uncials). The first Bibles containing both the Old Testament (OT) and the New Testament (NT) are manuscript codices written in uncial, or majuscule, script (i.e. using capital letters). The three earliest are Codex Vaticanus (B), Codex Sinaiticus (S, or ℵ) and Codex Alexandrinus (A).

1. *Vaticanus,* from the fourth century CE, is foundational, for most books, as a prime textual witness to the original LXX. The manuscript has accidentally lost much of Genesis but is otherwise complete for the OT. It is relatively free from major revision (though not in Isaiah

or Judges), which is why it is usually taken as the default text for editions based on one particular manuscript.

2. *Sinaiticus*, also fourth century CE, unfortunately survives only in part, and lacks most of the Pentateuch and the historical books. Where extant, it is often a reasonably reliable witness to an unrevised LXX.

3. *Alexandrinus*, fifth century CE, is very nearly complete. It is idiosyncratic, and marked by revisions, but it is often an important witness to very early readings; for instance, it offers the most reliable text for Isaiah.

Other manuscripts. These three manuscripts are supplemented by many other important uncials, and by a great number of cursive, or minuscule, manuscripts (i.e. written in small letters). The cursives range in date from the ninth century CE until the advent of printing and are by far the more numerous. They are generally given less weight in the task of trying to restore the text of the LXX, but sometimes they preserve ancient readings; each manuscript must be weighed on its merits.

In order therefore to produce a reliable text of the LXX, as near to the original translation as possible, the textual editor must consider many kinds of evidence, from the pre-Christian papyri to the late medieval cursives.

Printed editions

Early editions. Several developments that contributed to modern practice occurred in the period following the invention of printing in the fifteenth century. The Reformation led to a renewed emphasis on the Hebrew Bible. Where the inerrancy of Scripture was an issue, it was clearly essential to know that texts translated into the vernacular were reliable. With the suspicion that some readings in the Hebrew Bible might be inaccurate, interest in the LXX revived, this time as a tool for establishing the Hebrew text through the sifting and evaluating of different manuscripts. Ironically, this was the very opposite of Origen's concern in the third century CE, to adjust the LXX to the Hebrew text.

With the Renaissance came a revival of interest in the LXX, mainly antiquarian, and the collection of manuscripts began in the Vatican, in other centres of learning and in private collections. The invention of printing led to the production not just of the first Hebrew and vernacular Bibles, but also of the first great polyglots: the Complutensian (Alcalà, Spain, 1514–17, published 1520), the Aldine (Venice, 1519/20) and the Sixtine (Rome, 1587), which all included texts of the LXX. Here, it became clear that choices had to be made in the use of manuscripts, though at first it was probably a matter of what was locally available. But in the case of the Sixtine there was a deliberate decision to use Vaticanus, whenever possible, as being the most reliable source. As the importance of Vaticanus became apparent to textual critics, the Sixtine became the most widely used edition. This practice lasted until the advent of the first critical editions, beginning with Grabe's, published between 1707 and 1720 and based on Alexandrinus. It culminated with the great edition of Holmes and Parsons, published between 1798 and 1827 and based on Vaticanus, which had very full critical apparatuses. It was at this time also that the apocryphal books began to be grouped together at the end of Bibles, a radical departure from earlier practice. In the Holmes Parsons edition of 1827, for instance, they were published last, as Volume V.

Modern editions. Modern critical editions are of two kinds, 'diplomatic' or 'reconstructed'.

1. *Diplomatic editions.* These print the text of one particular manuscript (usually Vaticanus), and present evidence from other witnesses (manuscripts, patristic quotations, etc.) in a critical apparatus, so that readers can do their own textual criticism. Swete's edition of 1887–94 is an example. The so-called 'Larger Cambridge Septuagint' of Brooke, McLean and Thackeray (1906–40) adopted this method; this edition is still widely used by scholars,

especially for books not yet covered by the Göttingen Septuagint (see Jobes and Silva 2000: 72, n. 2).

2. *Reconstructed editions.* These print a text already corrected by the editor to give what seems to be the best reading for each disputed case; the evidence is supplied in the apparatus so that the reader can assess and, if need be, reject the reading chosen. Rahlfs (1935) and the Göttingen Septuagint adopt this method (see Jobes and Silva 2000: 75, 313–14). A reconstructed text is sometimes called 'eclectic'. The term is misleading because normally a default text is still used, and the alterations are the result of meticulous textual criticism (including emendations), not just patching together readings from different manuscripts. It is true, however, that the critically restored text does not correspond to any one extant manuscript; the critical apparatuses are, therefore, an essential feature.

Scholars differ as to which of the two types of critical text – the diplomatic or the reconstructed – is preferable, but in practice most use the reconstructed texts, where these are available, since, at least for the time being, they are the best approximations to the presumed original translations.

Secondary sources: the Christian versions

As well as the manuscript evidence, there are other sources for establishing the LXX's identity at the beginning of its history. Of these, possible quotations in early Jewish writings, in the NT and in other early Christian literature are of prime importance; they will be considered in Chapter 7. Another important source, the 'versions' (that is, early translations of the LXX into other languages), will be briefly considered here (some Jewish revisions or retranslations from the Hebrew, also called 'versions', will be discussed in Chapter 5).

From the second century CE onwards the Greek LXX, now established as the Christian Bible, itself needed to be translated for readers who did not know Greek. The earliest of these translations are the Old Latin version (OL, also known as the Vetus Latina, VL), from North Africa and Italy, and the Coptic versions from Egypt. They are of particular value in reflecting a state of the Greek text sometimes nearer the presumed original than the major manuscripts. For information on all the other early versions, see 'Further reading' at the end of this chapter.

The Old Latin

Although in the Hellenistic period Greek was the *lingua franca* of the Mediterranean world, the expansion of the Roman Empire led to the diffusion of Latin as well (and the north-western limits – parts of Gaul, for instance – were never predominantly Greek-speaking). Outside Italy the North African churches, especially Carthage, used Latin. From the mid-second century CE onwards, Christian writers, beginning with Tertullian (c. 160–220) and Cyprian of Carthage (200–258), were using Latin versions of the LXX. As the OL is already marked in places by signs of revisional activity, these versions must have been made earlier in the second century, if not before this. The citations in these early writers, as well as the manuscript evidence itself (from the fifth century CE onwards in both an African and a European textual form) point to a complex history that is difficult to unravel, especially as the manuscript evidence is often incomplete or has not yet been critically edited.

The OL versions are important in several ways. They are witnesses to an early need for vernacular Scriptures. They give modern scholars some access to the text of the LXX before it had undergone systematic revision. They are translations made directly from the Greek, without much concern to make adjustments against the Hebrew. And they were made a century before Origen's systematic revision resulted in the obscuring of earlier forms of the Greek text. Eventually the Latin Vulgate, based on Jerome's translations from the Hebrew, replaced the OL for most books of the Bible. The Vulgate Psalms, however, are a revision, by Jerome, of the earlier OL version, and the OL survives substantially in apocryphal works for which Jerome had no Hebrew original (Wisdom, Sirach, Baruch and Maccabees). Where the text of the OL can be established, it is of great value for indicating ancient readings sometimes different from both the mainstream LXX witnesses and the MT.

The Coptic

These Egyptian versions go back to the third century CE, a time when Christianity is presumed to have spread from cosmopolitan Greek-speaking cities like Alexandria, where the LXX had probably originated, into more rural areas. Here, Coptic (the word is a corruption of 'Egyptian', from Greek *Aiguptios*, Swete 1914: 105) was spoken in a number of dialects, especially Sahidic, Bohairic and Akhmimic. The translations were written in an uncial script based on Greek, and contained many Greek loan words. Translation into Coptic may have begun in the second century, but the earliest evidence comes from the late-third-century Papyrus Bodmer 6, and from clues in later Egyptian Christian literature. The Sahidic and the later Bohairic versions are independent translations from the LXX (the Akhmimic is a version of the Sahidic). The Minor Prophets in the Sahidic version presuppose a revised form of the LXX similar in places to that of 8HevXIIgr (see above, p. 4) and known from at least the late-first century BCE (see Bogaert 1993: 632–3; Fernández Marcos 2000: 347–50).

The content of the Septuagint

As well as witnessing to the text of the LXX, the early uncials show how the biblical collections were arranged, and which books they contained. While texts were copied onto individual papyrus rolls, we can hardly talk about canonical order for biblical books. Evidence for grouping and sequence comes from discussions in authors such as Josephus (*Apion* 1.39–42), Melito of Sardis and Origen (in Eusebius, *Historia Ecclesiae* (*HE*) 4.26.14; 6.25.2). But once the codex came into general use, choices had to be made as to which book should be permanently bound next to which. The earliest Christian

Bibles suggest a different understanding of the interrelation-
ship between the books from that reflected in Jewish writings
(complete Hebrew Bibles appear only in the ninth and tenth
centuries CE). They also reveal differences among the
Christian churches. These point to varying perceptions of
what counted as a scriptural book, making it unlikely that
there was ever a single 'Alexandrian (i.e. Septuagint) Canon'
as such.

Differences between Hebrew and Greek order

(1) Torah/Pentateuch. There never seems to have been any
deviation in the order of the five books attributed to Moses in
either Hebrew or Greek, and they always come first. This
points to the antiquity and high status of the collection.

(2) Hebrew arrangement of other books. Jewish sources designate as
'Former Prophets' the books of Joshua, Judges, 1–2 Samuel
and 1–2 Kings, and as 'Latter Prophets' Isaiah, Jeremiah,
Ezekiel and the Minor Prophets (though not always in that
order). The rest of the Hebrew canonical books are grouped
together as 'The Writings'; Hebrew manuscripts display some
variation in the order.

(3) Greek arrangement of other books. The Greek Bibles seem to
reflect an understanding of the 'Former Prophets' as histories
and often associate other apparently historical works with
them. Hence, Ruth is usually placed between Judges and 1
Samuel. 1 and 2 Samuel and 1 and 2 Kings are called 1 and 2
Kingdoms (or Reigns) and 3 and 4 Kingdoms (Reigns)
respectively. 4 Kingdoms is sometimes followed immediately
by 1 and 2 Chronicles (Paraleipomenōn, the books of 'things
left over') and often by 1 and 2 Esdras (1 Esdras is a
pseudepigraphical work only included in some manuscripts; 2
Esdras corresponds to the Hebrew books of Ezra and
Nehemiah). Some manuscripts also include at this point one
or more of the four books of Maccabees. Esther is often
accompanied by Judith and Tobit. Then, instead of moving to
the prophetic books, some manuscripts have a large section

containing all the remaining books found in the Hebrew 'Writings' with, usually, several of the other apocryphal books, especially Sirach and the Wisdom of Solomon. This arrangement seems to be by reason of the poetic or (especially) the sapiential nature of the books. The Christian character of 'the LXX' in the complete Bibles is shown by the frequent addition, after the Psalms, of a collection of 'Odes', including NT as well as OT liturgical 'canticles'. There is, however, much variation in order. Although there were early debates about the canonicity of various books, the manuscripts – as already noted – do not separate apocryphal and pseudepigraphical books from canonical ones (Swete 1914: 201 gives the placings in B, S and A).

The prophetic corpus in the Christian Bibles differs from that of Hebrew Bibles in placing Daniel with the three major prophets, usually after Ezekiel, though sometimes before (perhaps with a chronological concern, cf. Ezek. 14.14, 20; see Bogaert 1993: 646). Lamentations follows Jeremiah; and the first six of the twelve Minor Prophets are in the order Hosea, Amos, Micah, Joel, Obadiah, Jonah (8ḤevXIIgr follows the Hebrew order). Hebrew Bibles seem to put the prophets from Hosea to Micah in supposed chronological order, while the Greek, at least in Vaticanus, has a descending order of length. The whole corpus is sometimes arranged in a different order from that usual in modern Bibles. The Minor Prophets, for instance, sometimes precede the other prophetic books. Apocryphal Greek material also appears, attached to the books of Jeremiah (Baruch, Letter of Jeremiah) and of Daniel (Song of the Three Young Men, Prayer of Azariah, Susanna, Bel and the Dragon).

The individual books of the Septuagint

Each of the translations and original compositions that eventually constituted the Greek Bibles has its own history and character. In this final section we will look, inevitably briefly and selectively, at all the individual books (except *Wisdom of Solomon* and *Psalms of Solomon*), to situate their

particular interest for Septuagint study. This sometimes
primarily concerns their textual character and history, including their relationship, where appropriate, with the Hebrew
counterparts, sometimes other major areas of translational,
exegetical or cultural interest. The books are presented in the
order found in Rahlfs 1935, that is, with the apocryphal works
integrated.

The Pentateuch

1. *Genesis.* It is widely assumed that this was the first book to
   be translated into Greek; this is very likely, although
   there is no absolute external proof (it is already assumed
   by Philo, De Vita Mosis 2.37; see below, Chapter 4, p. 67).
   Genesis has therefore attracted a great deal of scholarly
   attention. The translation contains many interesting
   linguistic and exegetical solutions to challenges and
   difficulties in the Hebrew, as the translator strives to
   create something for which there is no exact precedent.
   He – the pronoun is doubtless appropriate (see de
   Troyer 1997: 333) – evidently aims to translate the
   Hebrew accurately. The text he is using is very similar to
   (though not always identical with) the later MT; it was, of
   course, unvocalized. He produces a Greek which is
   sometimes elegant and idiomatic, sometimes apparently
   influenced by Hebrew expressions and syntax. His
   practice is not always consistent, but this is understandable in someone who is, perhaps, feeling his way
   step by step. A detailed exegesis of 4.1–8 is given in Jobes
   and Silva (2000: 206–15).

2. *Exodus.* This translator is often quite adventurous in
   rendering the Hebrew; his translational style shows he is
   not the same as the Genesis translator. There are no
   major differences from the MT except in chapters 35–40
   (the second tabernacle account), which are shorter in
   the LXX and partly in a different order. There is no
   consensus as to how this has come about. It could be the
   result of differences in the translator's Hebrew text. Or it
   may be the work of a different translator. Or the same

translator may have chosen to depart from the original for interpretational reasons (see Wade 2003). There are many other points of exegetical interest throughout the book. Chapters 12–23, for instance, have been shown to have points of interpretation in common with some early rabbinic traditions (Büchner 1997).

3. *Leviticus.* This translator (different again) displays variety in the way he renders recurring Hebrew expressions, while remaining close to the original; he creates new idioms where necessary, especially when finding Greek equivalents for the technical cultic terms in which the book abounds.

4. *Numbers.* This translator has a less varied style and is usually fairly literal (especially where syntax is concerned), though he too sometimes translates rather freely, especially with regard to lexical choices. For cultic items, however, he often follows apparently established conventions. Unlike the previous translators, he does not take much account of the wider context, that is, his choices are determined by the immediate words to be translated, without cross-referencing (for a striking example of this feature in Genesis, see below, Chapter 6, p. 123).

5. *Deuteronomy.* The translator here is more aware of context, bringing different passages into line with each other. He is concerned with halakic matters (that is, with the correct observance of the law). Sometimes he appears to 'update' his translation. In 23.18, for instance, he apparently adds initiation into the Greek mysteries to the list of forbidden practices. He too translates rather literally and his Greek is less polished and innovative than that, say, of the Genesis or Exodus translators. Other interesting passages include 6.4, where the *Shema'* is preceded by an echo of 4.45 (perhaps associating 6.4 with the Decalogue), and 32.43 (the end of the Song of Moses). This has expansions similar to 4Q31(4QDeut^d; see Fernández Marcos 2000: 73; Dogniez and Harl 1992:

320, 340–1). These and other fragments found at Qumran point to the existence of other forms of the Hebrew text similar to those used by the translator.

6. *Summary.* Apart from the evidence it provides for different translators for each of the five books, LXX Pentateuch is significant for the influence which its vocabulary and translational style can be seen to have had on many other books. And if the Pentateuch was indeed the first part of the Hebrew Scriptures to be translated, it is also important for what it reveals of the theological and cultural milieu in which it arose.

The historical books

1. *Joshua.* This book well illustrates the effect of revisions on the manuscript tradition. The two main manuscripts, Vaticanus and Alexandrinus, are so different in 15.21b–62; 18.22–19.45 (passages concerning the territories of Judah, Benjamin and Simeon) that Rahlfs (1935) prints both versions. Some Hebrew manuscripts from Qumran reveal a text similar to that used by the translator, and often reflected in Vaticanus. The LXX omits 20.4–6 (on the cities of refuge), but adds several lines at the end of the book (24.33a–b), taken from various parts of Judges, apparently making a deliberate link with that book.

2. *Judges.* This book too witnesses to a very complex textual history; Rahlfs (1935) prints the text of both Vaticanus and Alexandrinus throughout. Neither manuscript reveals an unrevised form of the LXX, although each preserves some original elements. The text of Alexandrinus is marked by Origen's hexaplaric revision, while Vaticanus here witnesses to an earlier type of Hebraizing revision known as *kaige*. The so-called Antiochian manuscripts (or Antiochene; also known as Lucianic, see below, Chapter 5, p. 103) and the OL are probably the best witnesses to the original LXX of Judges.

3. *Ruth.* This book seems to have *kaige* features too as part of the original translation. For that reason it is considered one of the later translations, dated to the first century BCE/CE. But it is not always classed with the most literal translations and some recent work has detected signs of a more contextually motivated approach to the translation (see Wade 2000: 73–4).

4. *1–4 Kingdoms (Samuel-Kings).* As with Judges, the textual history is extremely complicated. Its importance lies particularly in the part it has played in the identification of a distinctive Antiochian text-type. In places it is likely that the Hebrew version used by the translators differed in content and arrangement, as well as actual wording, from the MT; the discovery at Qumran of 4Q51(4QSam^a) has confirmed the existence of this kind of text for 1–2 Kingdoms. In some places the LXX is longer than the MT, in others shorter, especially in 1 Kingdoms 17–18 (David and Goliath). In 1 Kingdoms 2 (the Song of Anna), the LXX omits vv. 8–9a, then adds verses modelled on Jeremiah 9.22–3. 3 and 4 Kingdoms diverge significantly from the MT, especially in the sections on Solomon, Jeroboam and Ahab, where there are some major expansions known as 'miscellanies'. These mainly consist of material that has been rearranged from elsewhere in the books, and they may reflect the translator's own exegetical reworkings. Among them are two contradictory résumés of the accession of Jeroboam (3 Kingdoms 12), perhaps reflecting two traditions about the schism, only one of which appears in the MT.

5. *1–2 Paraleipomenōn (1–2 Chronicles).* There are a few significant pluses and minuses, but no radical differences from the MT. Of major interest is the 'free' translational style which suggests a Jewish translator at home in the Greek world (on 'literal' and 'free' translations, see below, Chapter 6, pp. 119–21).

6. *1 and 2 Esdras.* 1 Esdras is interesting for its content. It combines rather free and elegant translation of parts of Hebrew Ezra and Nehemiah with a narrative, otherwise unknown, set in the court of Darius, King of Persia (3.1–5.6). Similarities have been seen with the vocabulary and style of LXX Daniel. 2 Esdras has sometimes been linked to the translator of Paraleipomenōn, but this is unlikely as 2 Esdras is much more literal in style. If, as seems probable, 1 Esdras came first, 2 Esdras may have been a deliberate attempt to produce a translation closer to a Hebrew text like that of the MT. But the relationship between 1 and 2 Esdras is far from clear.

7. *Esther.* The text has survived in two distinct forms, LXX and Alpha Text (AT, or L). There is much debate about the relationship between the two, which both have additions (A–F) not found in the MT. Possibly the OL represents a form of the text older than either the LXX or the AT; at any rate, it has distinctive elements including, some have thought, the playing-down of the anti-Gentile sentiments that appear in some of the additions. Among other interesting features, the additions mention God, famously not named in the MT of Esther. It is not clear whether they have been translated from lost Semitic originals or composed directly in Greek. In genre, Greek Esther has been likened to the romantic 'novels' which were popular in the Hellenistic period (Boyd-Taylor 1997; Wills 2002: 27–30). An exegesis of 5.1–2 with Addition D is given by Jobes and Silva (2000: 227–35).

8. *Judith.* Like 1 Esdras, this book has been associated in style with LXX Daniel. The OL sometimes witnesses to a form of the text not found in the Greek manuscripts.

9. *Tobit.* Like Esther, Tobit circulated in more than one form. The two most important forms are known as G^I and G^{II}. G^{II} is the earlier, reflected in manuscripts of Tobit in Hebrew found at Qumran. It is G^I, however, that occurs in most LXX manuscripts; it is shorter and seems

to be an early revision of G^{II}, which is found only in Sinaiticus and OL. It probably became more popular than the earlier version because of its improved literary qualities.

10. *1–4 Maccabees.* Each book is a separate work, with its own character. 1 Maccabees is a translation, though the source-text has not survived for comparison. 2 Maccabees is a Greek composition, an abridged version of an originally longer work, now lost. 3 Maccabees, a racy, popular story (about the Jews in Egypt rather than the Maccabees in Palestine), has a Greek style probably closer to the vernacular of Egypt, with some unusual vocabulary (this is 'normalized' against Septuagintal usage in Antiochian texts). 4 Maccabees, a philosophical and paraenetic work, is more literary in its language and style.

The sapiential books

1. *Psalms.* This was a very influential book, much quoted in the NT and subsequent Christian writings. Some psalms are divided differently from the MT, resulting in different numbering from 9 to 147 (MT 10–148), and there is an additional Psalm 151, quite different from the others; a similar Hebrew version has been found at Qumran. There are a number of additional or expanded headings. Some of these are liturgical, but most are historicizing, especially about David. Some scholars think that the 'historical' expansions are subsequent to the original translation. On the whole, the translator follows his source-text closely. The translation is thought by some to have influenced later Hebraizing translations and revisions in other books. Some scholars, however, demonstrate that the translation is less literalistic than often thought and that it contains many interpretational elements as well as stylistic devices that reveal a sophisticated rather than a mechanical approach to translation.

2. *Proverbs.* Textually, there are a number of substantial pluses over against the MT. These mostly come from elsewhere in the LXX and there is debate about whether they are the work of the translator or reflect an already adapted Hebrew text. Some touches, unlikely to have been found in a Hebrew source-text, may even point to a non-biblical origin (compare, for instance, 6.8a and Aristotle's *Historia Animalium* 622B; see Jobes and Silva 2000: 304). Chapters 24–9 have been rearranged, probably by the translator himself. LXX Proverbs stands out for its translational style, which is often free and paraphrastic. But although the translator contemporizes and even occasionally uses Greek poetic forms, his theological outlook has been identified as traditional, even conservative, a very interesting combination (see Cook 1997: 318–19; 2001).

3. *Ecclesiastes (Qoheleth); Song of Songs.* These two books are so literal in their translational style that, like Ruth, they have been associated with the Hebraizing *kaige* group of the first century BCE/CE. LXX Ecclesiastes has, in fact, sometimes been attributed to the early-second century CE Jewish translator Aquila, whose consistently literal translation is very distinctive (see below, Chapter 5, pp. 87–9). Although the book surely belongs to that line of development, direct authorship by Aquila is now thought unlikely. It is probable that, as with Ruth, more careful analysis of stylistic and contextual features will show that there are subleties, so far unnoticed, to the translation of both Ecclesiastes and Song of Songs.

4. *Job.* The LXX is shorter than the MT by 389 verses, though there are interesting midrashic additions at the end (42.17a–e). Debates continue as to whether the translator used a shorter Hebrew version, such as is now attested at Qumran, or whether he abridged the work himself to make it more palatable to a cultured audience, perhaps non-Jewish as well as Jewish, and to tone down some of Job's more shocking outbursts. He was clearly a cultured man

himself, and renders the difficult Hebrew in a free
and sometimes elegant Greek style.

5. *Sirach (Ben Sira/Ecclesiasticus).* The book is a translation of
a Hebrew composition. A unique feature is a Greek
prologue which allows both the original work and its
translation to be dated with some certainty. It also
establishes the translator as the author's grandson, thus
providing the only autobiographical evidence we have
for the identity and circumstances of a translator
(though even here he remains anonymous). This
prologue is of great interest for the translator's views
on the difficulties of translation, for the evidence it
provides of the range of biblical books by then translated
into Greek, and for its Greek style, more literary than the
book itself which is said to emulate a 'Septuagintal' style
(i.e. with many features close to Hebrew syntax and
idiom). Chapters 30.25–33.16a and 33.16b–36.10 have
been reversed – probably accidentally – in all extant
manuscripts (the amount of text affected shows that the
faulty copy must have been in codex form; Bogaert 1993:
628). The original order has been preserved by the OL,
as has been confirmed by the discovery of Hebrew
manuscripts of parts of Ben Sira. The possibility of
comparing Greek and Hebrew versions occurs only rarely
in the case of the apocryphal books, although, in this
case, the textual history of both traditions is immensely
complicated and not yet completely clear.

The prophetic books

1. *The Minor Prophets (Hosea-Malachi).* The first six books are
in a different order (above, p. 13) but otherwise the
Hebrew original seems to have been close to, though not
identical with, the MT. Five manuscripts do, however,
attest a different version of Habakkuk 3 closer to that of
the Jewish translator, Symmachus (Harl, Dorival and
Munnich 1988: 100, 180. LXX Hab. 3 itself diverges

more than chapters 1–2 from the Hebrew of the MT,
1988: 301). It seems likely that one person, or group,
translated the entire scroll. The source-text is followed
closely, but intelligently, usually in competent Greek.
There are many points of exegetical and theological
interest within these apparently literal translations which
repay careful study.

2. *Isaiah.* This translator is very distinctive. He renders a
text closely resembling the MT, but with considerable
freedom. There seems to be some historical updating in
places, presumably to show the translator's own generation that the prophecies apply to them (cf. Seeligmann
1948: 4, 82, 109), though the obscurity of much of the
original may have played its part too. Examples of
reinterpretation have been found in 1.26 (Jerusalem as
'metropolis'; Seeligmann 1948: 113–14), in chapter 14
(Assyria a cipher for Antiochus IV Epiphanes? Seeligmann 1948: 83–4; Bogaert 1993: 636), in 19.18 (a
favourable allusion to the Oniad temple at Leontopolis?
Seeligmann 1948: 68), and in 23.10 (a mention of
Carthage, though different conclusions are drawn as to
the significance; Harl, Dorival and Munnich 1988: 94–5);
and there are other similar passages. Like LXX Psalms,
LXX Isaiah had a great impact on the NT. LXX Isa. 6.9–
10, for example, which softens the shock of the Hebrew,
is put to apologetic use in Acts 28.27 (see Chapter 7, pp.
143–4). The so-called 'Servant Songs', which Christian
writers apply to Christ, are given a collective sense in the
LXX. For an exegesis of 52.13–53.12, see Jobes and Silva
(2000: 215–27).

3. *Jeremiah.* Textual questions dominate the study of LXX
Jeremiah. The LXX is 2,700 verses shorter than the MT;
4Q71(4QJer[b]) confirms the existence of a shorter
Hebrew text-form which presumably served as the
translator's model. This hypothesis now seems more
likely than the main alternative one, that the transla-
tor(s) deliberately abbreviated a longer Hebrew text
similar to the MT (see Soderlund 1985: 11–13 for

outlines). There is continuing debate as to which of the Hebrew editions was the earlier; the balance is probably in favour of the shorter form. As well as the difference in length, LXX Jeremiah has the 'Oracles Against the Nations' (MT 46–51) in a different place, and their internal ordering is different too. The LXX seems to stress the role of Baruch, whereas the MT focuses more exclusively on Jeremiah himself. Another focus of interest is on the number of translators: some think there were two, or even three (one of whom may have been the same as the translator of the Minor Prophets), others that there was only one whose work was partially revised, to mention only the two most influential hypotheses. Like Daniel, Jeremiah has attracted additional material written, or surviving, only in Greek (Baruch, Letter of Jeremiah).

4. *Ezekiel.* There are a number of differences in the content and order of some chapters. The discovery in 1931 of Papyrus 967 has helped clarify some of the issues, though others remain unclear, and some new problems have been created, especially the significance of 967's lack of 36.1–28a (the 'new heart' passage; also missing in one OL manuscript). The translator of the Minor Prophets may have had a hand in parts of Ezekiel too, though criteria for identifying different translators and for grouping translations are under review generally.

5. *Daniel.* Like Judges, Esther, Tobit and 1 and 2 Esdras, this is a 'double text', which eventually circulated in two distinct forms, the LXX and a version attributed to 'Theodotion' (Th). The latter, closer to the MT, ousted the LXX from all extant witnesses except one eleventh-century hexaplaric cursive (88), the seventh-century Syro-Hexaplar, and Papyrus 967. Rahlfs (1935) prints both versions. Papyrus 967 is the main witness to the original (pre-hexaplaric) LXX. Its arrangement of chapters 1–12 in the order 1–4; 7; 8; 5; 6; 9–12 produces a more logical regnal sequence and may go back to the original translation. The LXX is longer overall than the

MT, though it has minuses too. The style, especially in chapters 4–6, is lively and paraphrastic (see, for instance, the accounts of the fiery furnace and of Nebuchadnez-zar's madness). The relationship of the two versions to each other and to the MT is much debated (see further on 'Theodotion' in Chapter 5, pp. 84–7). The Greek additions to Daniel (Song of the Three Young Men, Prayer of Azariah, Susanna, Bel and the Dragon) made a great impact on later Christian exegesis, art and literature.

Summary

At the beginning of this chapter the question was asked, 'what is the LXX?' Attempts at definition have revealed a complex historical and textual reality and have shown the importance of distinguishing between the original translations and the manuscripts and editions in which these have come down to us. Taking 'Septuagint' in its broadest sense, we have looked at some of the features of the earliest Greek Bibles and of the individual books contained in them. We have seen how 'the LXX', understood as collections of sacred texts both like and unlike their Hebrew counterparts, has been transmitted through the centuries in manuscripts and printed editions. The next two chapters will investigate the historical origins of the first translations. As this investigation largely involves hypotheses of various kinds, it is important, at the start, not to lose sight of what, at the material level, the LXX 'is': a vast, diverse corpus of religious texts in Greek. Just how difficult it is to discern within this corpus the authentic features of the first translations will become evident as we proceed.

Further reading

For an extensive general introduction to supplement that of Jobes and Silva (2000), the handbook compiled by M. Harl, G. Dorival and O. Munnich in 1988 to accompany the first volumes of the BA is highly recommended. Useful shorter introductions include: Schürer (1986); Tov (1988); Peters (1992); Bogaert (1993).

For more detailed information, Swete (1914), although dated in some respects, still contains much material not found in the later introductions. Knowledge of Hebrew, Greek and Latin is, however, presupposed; there are no translations or transliterations. Jellicoe (1968) continues Swete's work and is also a valuable resource.

On the primary sources and their history, see Swete (1914: 122–94); Jellicoe (1968: 1–25, 176–242, 269–313); Kenyon (1975); Metzger (1981); Harl, Dorival and Munnich (1988: 129–36); Jobes and Silva (2000: 57–63). For the development of the codex, see Roberts (1970: 55–60).

On the versions, see Swete (1914: 87–121); Jellicoe (1968: 243–68); Kenyon (1975: 53–9); Harl, Dorival and Munnich (1988: 136–40); Fernández Marcos (2000: 346–61). Jobes and Silva (2000: 278–80) raise some methodological and text-critical questions.

On the LXX and the Dead Sea Scrolls, see Klein (1974: 11–26); Greenspoon (1998: 101–27); Jobes and Silva (2000: 169–71).

For questions of content and order, see Swete (1914: 200–2); Ackroyd and Evans (1970: 136–8, 140–2); for the Apocrypha, Goodman (2001: 618–19).

For further details on the individual books, see Swete (1914: 231–88); Jellicoe (1968: 272–300, especially the manuscript history); Harl, Dorival and Munnich (1988: 173–82); most recently Bogaert (1993: 577–650). For detailed bibliographies, consult Brock, Fritsch and Jellicoe (1973); Dogniez (1995). On the 'double texts', see Fernández Marcos (2000: 88–101).

CHAPTER 2

Origins: Facts and Fictions

Introduction

Evidence begins to accumulate for the existence of many books of the Hebrew Bible in Greek from the mid-second century BCE. By the end of the first century CE, wider collections were in circulation among both Greek-speaking Jews and Christians, some of them revised in various ways. By the time of the first nearly complete manuscripts in the fourth century, all the books of the LXX were established as Scripture in the Christian churches, although within Greek-speaking Judaism alternative versions, especially Aquila's, were also widely used.

So much seems clear. But can we trace the beginnings of the LXX further back than the second century BCE? Where and when were the first books translated? What do we know about the translators? Why were the translations undertaken at all? There is, in fact, very little that can be said with certainty in reply to any of these questions. At first glance this is surprising because we appear to have, in early Jewish sources, clear information at least for the Pentateuch. Historical details appear to be provided by the pseudonymous author of *The Letter of Aristeas to Philocrates* (*Ep. Arist.*) and other Jewish writers. *Ep. Arist.* claims that 'the divine Law' (3) of Moses was translated into Greek in Alexandria during the reign of Ptolemy II Philadelphus (285–246 BCE) to be put in the great library there; the work was done by experts brought for the purpose from Jerusalem. The Jewish philosopher Aristobulus

27

also refers to a systematic translation of the Law under Philadelphus. Although these second-century accounts are problematic and scholars no longer accept them as they stand, they continue to exert considerable influence on most, if not all, modern reconstructions. That is why we must first examine the early accounts, especially *Ep. Arist.*, before looking, in Chapter 3, at some current hypotheses.

The Letter of Aristeas

At face value, this entertaining but enigmatic work is an eye-witness account, by a pagan Greek at the court of Philadel-phus, of how seventy-two Jewish scholars were brought from Jerusalem to translate the Law into Greek for inclusion in the royal library at Alexandria. The consensus is, however, that the anonymous author was really a Jew writing not in the third but in the second century BCE. There is no agreement as to exactly when, but most current research points to the latter half of the century. The purpose of the work is disputed; it would be easier to decide were the dating more secure. Its mixture of literary genres adds to the difficulty: within the overall form of a letter it contains a narrative which itself includes a travelogue, a symposium and an apologia for the Law, to mention only a few elements; it should be remembered, however, that such mixtures are typical of Hellenistic literature, especially fiction. There is certainly more afoot than a simple account of the translation of the Law (it is never actually called the Pentateuch, nor is the content ever listed). The following brief outline brings out the salient points; for an alternative analysis emphasizing the oddities, see Goldstein (1991: 1–7); for editions, discussions on dating and other issues, see the end of this chapter.

Outline of content

1–8	Prologue. Aristeas offers his friend Philocrates (and other like-minded people) an edifying 'narrative' (*diēgēsis*) about, first, the meeting with

the Jewish High Priest Eleazer to arrange for the translation of the Law and, second, his successful petition for the release of Jewish slaves, prisoners-of-war taken by Philadelphus's father. The narrative then begins.

9–12a   The royal librarian, Demetrius of Phalerum, suggests that the Jewish law-books are worth translating. Philadelphus authorizes a letter to the High Priest.

12b–27   Aristeas seizes his opportunity to plead, successfully, for the release of the slaves. One of his arguments is that the Law must be translated and expounded for the benefit of all.

28–32   Demetrius explains the necessity for the translation: the current Hebrew scrolls (or just possibly the existing Greek translations; the text is ambiguous) are inaccurate, due to lack of royal patronage.

33–40   Aristeas, and another courtier called Andreas, take an adulatory but firm letter from Philadelphus to Eleazer, stating that the Law is to be translated and placed with the other books in the library.

41–51   Eleazer writes an adulatory letter to Philadelphus acquiescing and giving the names of the seventy-two translators (six from each tribe).

52–82   A detailed description follows of all the ceremonial gifts Philadelphus had sent for the Temple, and their artistic merits.

83–120   This leads into an admiring description of the Temple, the High Priest's vestments, the city and countryside, and other details.

121–7   The translators are introduced as philosophers who will adorn Philadelphus's court. Their mission is to teach the Law correctly for the benefit of all citizens, since hearing is more effective than reading.

128–71   A demonstration of the true, rational, symbolic meaning of the Law is given: why Jews are monotheists, have food-laws, etc.

172–86   The narrative resumes: the travellers reach Alex-
          andria and are given immediate (and unprece-
          dented) audience by Philadelphus who does
          obeisance to the scrolls as containing divine
          oracles. He announces a banquet in honour of
          the translators at which he too will observe Jewish
          food-laws.

187–300   Prolonged account of the seven-day feast during
          which each of the translators is asked a question
          by Philadelphus and replies sagely. The questions
          are mainly concerned with how to rule wisely and
          successfully. Aristeas claims to have consulted the
          daily court-records for his verbatim account.

301–11   The work of translation is now undertaken in
          quietness and comfort on the 'island' (not
          actually named as Pharos). The translators discuss
          each verse and reach a consensus as they go along.
          They complete their task in seventy-two days, then
          hand their work to Demetrius to make a fair copy.
          Demetrius assembles the whole Jewish community
          and reads the Law to them. The leaders ask for a
          copy, which is formally acknowledged, and future
          revision is strictly forbidden.

312–21   Philadelphus reads the Law, is impressed, and
          orders the books to be treated with reverence. He
          sends the translators back to Eleazer with further
          gifts.

322   Epilogue. Aristeas promises to send Philocrates
          further edifying material.

Relevance to the Septuagint

Several points should be noted before this 'narrative' is used as
a source for dating and understanding LXX origins.

(1) Jewish character. 'Aristeas' himself, despite his veneer of
sympathetic paganism, clearly writes as a Jew with a Jewish
agenda.

(2) Historical background. The story is set in the reign of the second Ptolemy (285–246 BCE), but there are several historical inaccuracies. The most glaring is the presence of Demetrius of Phalerum who had been banished by Philadelphus soon after his accession and who is never referred to elsewhere as royal librarian.

There are also several improbabilities: the apparently non-Jewish Aristeas's working knowledge of Judaism; Philadelphus's relation of equality with Eleazer, and his excessive enthusiasm for all things Jewish; a hundred thousand Jewish slaves being emancipated to secure the translation of the Hebrew scrolls. On the other hand, there are authentic details about Ptolemaic court life and administration, although these need not point exclusively to the reign of Philadelphus. The various claims to quote from, or to have consulted, official documents are, however, literary devices, often found in this kind of quasi-historical romance, to give verisimilitude. The banquet with philosophical discussion is a well-established genre (cf. Plato's *Symposium*), here combined with 'the debate on the nature of kingship' (*peri basileiās*), also popular in Hellenistic writings (Fernández Marcos 2000: 38, 42). The portrait of Philadelphus as a generous patron of the arts does, however, ring true. His reign lived on in the literary imagination as a kind of golden age of culture (rather like the Elizabethan age in England) and thus provided a suitable setting, with perhaps some truth to it, for what the real (anonymous) author intended.

(3) Purpose. The author's intention is, however, difficult to pin down. The prologue suggests that the theme might be something like 'The Embassy to Eleazer' (1) or 'The Story of the Translating of the Divine Law' (3). But the emphasis is more on how the Law is to be interpreted and communicated, and on its ethical, rational, symbolic character (when expounded by experts), than on the actual process of translating, which is described only cursorily. That is, the 'why' of the translation is really more important than the 'when' or the 'where' or the 'how'. It is emphatically for instruction: the Law is not only to be translated but

expounded, and for the benefit of the whole community. The impression emerges of a group either proud of its integration into educated Greek society, or needing to have its self-image affirmed, or perhaps a mixture of both; hence the importance, even if in fictional terms, of the patronage and admiration not only of Philadelphus, but also of Demetrius, a well-known philosopher and ex-ruler of Athens. The historical blunder may have been deliberate.

(4) Main emphases. There are at least two apparent interests. First, there is the emphasis on Jerusalem, the High Priest, the Temple and its ceremonies (expressed, perhaps, in the enthusiastic language of occasional visitors or pilgrims), and the Judaean philosopher-translators, all as arbiters of excellence. Great pride is displayed in Jewish religion and culture, exemplified in the way in which Eleazer and Philadelphus are portrayed as equals.

Secondly, Philadelphus is shown as supremely benevolent towards the Jews and appreciative of them, with a clear unspoken message that the Ptolemies are worthy rulers. This may have seemed necessary in the second century BCE when Ptolemaic rule was threatened, especially by the Seleucids of Syria, and political loyalties, including those of Jews, were divided.

'Aristeas' is thus wholeheartedly in favour both of enlightened Judaism, in harmony with Jerusalem, and of Ptolemaic rule. His story of the translation of the law brings these two elements together as equally important components of Egyptian Judaism. The LXX functions as a vehicle for showing how well Alexandrian Judaism integrates its traditional 'divine law' into its contemporary situation.

(5) Defence of the LXX? A further motive for using the translation as the framing story may be to defend the traditional LXX from contemporary pressures to revise it against a particular form of the Hebrew text, or against revisions actually in existence; the Oniad temple at Leontopolis is often suggested as the locus for such a rival version, but this is entirely hypothetical. There is, of course,

some manuscript evidence for at least retouchings of the texts from the second century BCE onwards, though these hardly amount to full-scale alternative versions. But *Ep. Arist.* may perhaps be a clever way of resisting pressure (if it really existed) by presenting the original versions as the work of Jerusalem experts. But it cannot have been the only intention of the work, because the portrait of Philadelphus and his treatment of the Jews indicates a wider and more political agenda.

(6) Summary. Ep. Arist. is an important Hellenistic Jewish work, though less useful for LXX origins than is usually supposed. Its importance lies more in the glimpse it gives of attitudes towards an already established translation, and of methods of exegesis and instruction in at least one diaspora community. Goldstein sums up the message as, 'Obey the Torah, Venerate the Temple of Jerusalem, but speak Greek and Put your Hopes in the Ptolemaic Dynasty' (1991: 1, 18). Philadelphus's request for a copy of the Jewish laws then functions primarily as the narrative excuse for a demonstration of Jewish wisdom and loyalty. The work may transmit genuine information, but this cannot be verified. It is perhaps prudent not to start discussions about the date and origin of the LXX from *Ep. Arist.* but to use this narrative for possible back-up (just as traditions preserved in later Christian writings may give weight to other arguments about the origins of the New Testament Gospels, but would not now be used as starting points for establishing these origins). Tov's approach is to be recommended: he looks first at evidence within the LXX itself (and finds very little; only that the Pentateuch is a Jewish work, whose vocabulary points to Egypt and to a variety of translators) before discussing *Ep. Arist.* and other writings (1988: 164).

Aristobulus

Sources

The writings of this interesting early apologist for the compatibility of Jewish faith and Greek philosophy survive in only a few fragments. Extracted from the work of the non-Jewish writer Alexander Polyhistor (first century BCE), they are quoted by the Christian writers Clement of Alexandria and Eusebius of Caesarea (third and fourth centuries CE respectively). Eusebius incorporates Clement's material, with some additions from Anatolius of Laodicea (d. 282 CE). The fragments are of inherent interest for what they reveal about Hellenistic Jewish culture and as examples of an allegorical approach to the interpretation of Scripture more fully developed by Philo (see Chapter 7, pp. 140–1).

Aristobulus on the Septuagint

The only reference to the LXX comes in Fragment 3, in the context of a demonstration by Aristobulus that Pythagoras, Plato and other Greeks took their best ideas from earlier, partial versions of the Mosaic law: 'before the dominion of Alexander and the Persians, others had translated (*diērmēneutai ... di'heterōn*) accounts of the events surrounding the exodus from Egypt of the Hebrews, our countrymen, and the disclosure to them of all the things that had happened as well as their domination of the land, and the detailed account of the entire law...' (Eusebius, *Praeparatio Evangelica* (*PE*) 13.12.1; translation by Holladay 1995: 152–5). The passage continues: 'but the complete translation of everything in the law occurred at the time of the king surnamed Philadelphus ... who brought great zeal to this undertaking, while Demetrius of Phalerum attended to matters relating to these things' (13.12.2; Holladay 1995: 157).

Clement's version is fuller: 'it is said that the Scriptures both of the law *and the prophets* were translated from the dialect of the Hebrews into the Greek language in the reign of *Ptolemy the son of Lagus*, or, according to some, in the time of Ptolemy surnamed Philadelphus, when Demetrius of Phalerum brought to this task the greatest zeal, [and] attended to the matters of translation with painstaking accuracy' (*Stromateis* 1.22.148; Holladay 1995: 157; emphases added).

There are two suspicious elements here: the addition of 'and the prophets', since these books were not translated until later, and the uncertainty over the Ptolemy involved ('the son of Lagus' is Ptolemy I Soter). As in *Ep. Arist.*, Demetrius of Phalerum is anachronistically associated with Philadelphus, although, in Eusebius's version, Aristobulus gives Demetrius a role subordinate to that of the king (but see Holladay 1995: 217, n. 85 for textual uncertainties in both Eusebius and Clement here). This may be because Aristobulus is addressing a descendant of Philadelphus; he is not named, but Clement's identification with Ptolemy VI Philometor (180–145 BCE) is generally accepted (*Stromateis* 1.22.150; Holladay 1995: 151). This situates Aristobulus in the mid-second century BCE, but one should remain aware that the identification, and with it the date, is not absolutely certain.

Earlier versions of the Septuagint?

Is Aristobulus correct in speaking of the existence of other, partial, versions before the time of Philadelphus? Most scholars reject the claim on the grounds that it reflects an attempt, for apologetic reasons, to show that Plato, and other Greeks, had access to Jewish sources (elsewhere he even includes Orpheus, as well as Homer and Hesiod, among those who took their ideas from the Jews; Eusebius *PE* 13.12.4, 13; Holladay 1995: 165, 189). This is doubtless correct, but Aristobulus may all the same have known of early attempts at rendering the Exodus story and other very significant portions into Greek, even if these were nothing like as old as he claims. Some scholars argue, however, that the word *diērmēneutai* refers not to translations but to narrative 'rewritings' such as are found in Demetrius the Historian and other early Jewish authors (see Chapter 7, pp. 136–8). This is also possible. It is, in any case, striking that Genesis does not seem to be included and that if 'conquest of the land' refers to the book of Joshua (rather than Deuteronomy), more than the Torah is involved (Holladay 1995: 215; see also Garbini 1988: 136–8).

Relationship between Aristobulus and The Letter of Aristeas

There are three possibilities for Aristobulus's relationship with *Ep. Arist.*: each author drew independently on existing traditions; *Ep. Arist.* drew on Aristobulus; Aristobulus drew on *Ep. Arist.* Scholars are divided on this question, with a tendency now to opt for an independent use of common tradition, or an even more agnostic stance.

1. *Independent use of traditions.* If the two writers drew on common material, there is no necessary dependence of one on the other, and Aristobulus cannot be used for establishing the date of *Ep. Arist.* (or vice versa). But unless there was an earlier elaborate account now lost, it seems unlikely that the linking of Demetrius with Philadelphus existed before the author of *Ep. Arist.* made capital out of it; the analysis of *Ep. Arist.* (above, pp. 28–30) has shown that this scenario was important for the author's literary and ideological purposes. It is quite likely that traditions existed, but the nature of the shared material here is suspicious.

2. Ep. Arist. *depends on Aristobulus.* If *Ep. Arist.* draws on Aristobulus, the second part of the second century BCE is indicated for the composition of the story, which would be a vastly elaborated version arising out of Aristobulus's meagre details. Those who opt for this relationship argue that it is more likely that *Ep. Arist.* has embroidered than that Aristobulus has reduced the material. This is not a particularly strong argument and leaves out of account the context in which Aristobulus refers to the LXX. His comment is a passing allusion to highlight his real interest in the alleged earlier sources for the Greek philosophers; he is not concerned with the LXX as such. Bartlett's objection (1985: 17) that *Ep. Arist.*, not Aristobulus, always appears in subsequent sources as the originator of the LXX legend can be discounted: Aristobulus's references are so minimal that, even if they came first, they lack substance to fire the collective imagination in the way that *Ep. Arist.* did.

3. *Aristobulus depends on* Ep. Arist. In this case, the argument is reversed: Aristobulus has taken from *Ep. Arist.* the minimum of information needed for his own argument

and has not bothered about the rest. This is not unlikely, and there are other considerations which reinforce the plausibility. First, according to Eusebius (above, pp. 34–5), he is at pains to put Demetrius in his place as the one who carried out Philadelphus's project. This contrasts with *Ep. Arist.* where Demetrius plays a more prominent part, and suggests that Aristobulus may be attempting to set the record straight, or at least to tell the story in the way in which the king his patron will expect. One should note, however, that Clement's version is less clear on the relationship, and that, immediately before the words quoted above, Eusebius credits Aristobulus with saying 'For it [the law] had been translated by others before Demetrius of Phalerum...' This, together with the reputation of Philadelphus for generosity, is enough to explain the compliment paid by Aristobulus. But it is also possible that he may have picked up the rather odd remark in *Ep. Arist.* 30, that former attempts to translate the Law had failed because they lacked royal patronage. Aristobulus's statement makes it clear that royal patronage was indeed forthcoming and resulted in the translation of the 'whole Law'.

Aristobulus in context

If we are to risk any decision on relationship between the two writings, the third option seems the most likely. That means that if Aristobulus wrote sometime between 170 and 150 BCE, *Ep. Arist.* must predate the time of composition, giving an earlier date than is usual today. But it must be remembered that the identification of Aristobulus's patron as Philometor, though likely, is not certain.

Another factor contributing to the uncertainty is the nature of the work – 'the exposition of the laws of Moses', or whatever its original title was – from which only five extracts remain. It purports to be addressed directly to the king, and one passage uses the device of answering questions about the meaning of the Scriptures put by the king himself (Fragment 2, Eusebius *PE* 8.10.1–2; Holladay 1995: 135, 137). Even while conceding

that this is a common Hellenistic literary device, and also that
the explanations are aimed as much at fellow Jews as at a Greek
readership, most scholars take it for granted that the work
really was written for King Ptolemy and his court. We should
perhaps wonder about the likelihood of this, even allowing for
a marked pro-Jewish sympathy on the part of Philometor.
Aristobulus was credited with having been the king's *didaskalos*,
that is, his 'teacher' or 'tutor' (an official title). This comes in
2 Maccabees 1.10b, which addresses an Aristobulus who is also
a member of the high-priestly family in Egypt and a leader of
the Jewish community. The identification is usually accepted,
though it may be an instance of the tendency to equate people
of the same name.

But the fact that Aristobulus's work has survived only in
much later writers, whose reliability is not always to be trusted,
should make us cautious. Eusebius, for instance, quotes his
older contemporary Anatolius as saying that Aristobulus was
one of the original translators of the LXX, though there is no
one of that name in the list given in *Ep. Arist.* 47–51. There are
also contradictory statements from Clement. Dorival insists
that only what is directly quoted from Aristobulus about the
LXX should be relied on, and even that with caution.
Certainly, we should not press too hard for help in dating
Ep. Arist. (Harl, Dorival and Munnich 1988: 45–6; cf. Holladay
1995: 215). What is of greater interest is that we have a
different kind of witness to traditions about the LXX, again
linking them with the reign of Philadelphus, and giving the
LXX a prominent role in the religious and intellectual life of
diaspora Judaism.

Whatever their exact, and respective, dates, *Ep. Arist.* and
the Aristobulus fragments are the earliest and most restrained
accounts of the translation of the Jewish law (later elaborations
in Philo and some Christian authors will be discussed in
Chapter 4). They agree on situating it in the early-third
century BCE, as an initiative of Ptolemy. But, as we shall see in
the next chapter, even these claims are less secure than they
may seem.

Further reading

For Ep. Arist.

The literature is vast. A few items are given here; fuller bibliographies can be found in dictionary entries and specialized studies.

Thackeray's edition of the text in Greek (see Swete 1914: 533–606) is the one most commonly used. Meecham (1935) also has an edition. The Greek text with translation is given in Hadas (1951; this also has a commentary); Pelletier (1962). Translations only are given by Shutt (1985: 7–34); Thackeray (1917, with a useful appendix of 'Ancient Evidence on the Origins of the Septuagint').

Of the many surveys and discussions in print, Bartlett (1985: 11–34) has a useful introduction, with annotated selected readings. Gruen (1998: 206–22) is challenging and original. Murray (1967) has an important discussion. Shutt (1992: 380–2) and Sollamo (2001) are also useful.

For Aristobulus

The most accessible edition in English is Holladay (1995). It contains Greek text and English translation for all the fragments, as well as a detailed introduction and notes. For an introduction and translation only, see Yarbro Collins (1985: 831–42).

There are good short introductions in Holladay (1992: 383–4); Schürer (1986: 579–87); Walter (1989: 389–91); Winston (1999: 56–7). Borgen (1984: 233–82) has a longer treatment. Major surveys include Walter (1964; a foundational study); Winston (1996: 155–66).

For the identification in 2 Maccabees 1.10b, see Bartlett (1973: 5, 17, 223); Goldstein (1983: 157–69); Harl, Dorival and Munnich (1988: 45, 49, 67).

On Ptolemaic patronage and the library of Alexandria, see Fraser (1972: 305–35).

For the historical background of third- and second-century BCE Egypt, see Grabbe (1992a: 212–18; 270–307).

CHAPTER 3

Origins: Questions and Issues

Modern attempts to reconstruct LXX origins have concentrated on the Pentateuch, on the assumption that these books were the first to be translated. Hypotheses and issues in this area will, therefore, be considered first. Questions must then be asked about the translation of the remaining books. Matters of dating, geography and cultural milieu are important here, both for establishing the text of the LXX and for understanding its place in Hellenistic Judaism.

Dating, location and purpose

The translation of the Pentateuch

Dating
Most scholars opt for the early- to mid-third century BCE (*c.* 280–250 BCE). The following are the main arguments, with the problems they entail:

1. *Ep. Arist.* has at least some historical plausibility. The difficulties in determining a historical nucleus, arising from the work's literary genre and its author's agenda, have been noted in Chapter 2 (see above, p. 28).

2. Biblical quotations or allusions supposing knowledge of the LXX occur in Hellenistic Jewish writers from the end of the third century BCE onwards (Swete 1914: 369–70 gives a list). If the attributions are reliable, and if the biblical allusions are really based on the LXX, then this

evidence, though meagre, is precious. But certainty is difficult to establish (see Chapter 7, p. 136.

3. Other books of the LXX utilize the vocabulary of the Greek Pentateuch. This is important for relative dating but does not in itself clinch a date for the original translation.

4. The Greek of the Pentateuch reflects an identifiable stage in the development of Koine (the 'common' language of the Hellenistic period) consonant with the early-third century. This is probably the strongest argument, though it is doubtful how precise, as yet, the results can be (see below pp. 50–1).

Location

The setting of the initial enterprise in Alexandria has not been seriously challenged, though it should be remembered that there were other major cities with flourishing Jewish communities in Egypt (e.g. Memphis) and elsewhere in North Africa (e.g. Cyrene) and Asia Minor (e.g. Ephesus) which could conceivably have provided a suitable milieu.

Purpose

Views on the reason for the undertaking divide into two approaches: it was either a Greek initiative or a Jewish one.

(1) A Greek initiative. This approach posits a request for a translation of the Jewish law from either Ptolemy Philadelphus in person (as in *Ep. Arist.*) or from his administration. This is no longer the majority view, though Dorival considers royal interest possible, and Barthélemy defends a hypothesis, which goes back to Rost and is also argued by Mélèze-Modrzejewski, that Jewish law-texts in Greek were needed for administrative purposes (see Harl, Dorival and Munnich 1988: 72–8; Barthélemy 1974: 23–41). A number of scholars consider that some Ptolemaic interest in a Jewish initiative is plausible.

Dorival's argument is instructive for its presuppositions and the type of question it provokes. By analogy with the Aramaic Targums, he thinks it unlikely that the authorities in

Jerusalem, assumed to have control over the diaspora communities, would have countenanced written translations at this period, but had no choice except to bow to Ptolemy's request. But we may ask whether Jerusalem really exercised such control at this time or had this attitude to the use of Greek. From the available evidence, it seems unlikely.

Later rabbinic traditions (e.g. *b. Masseket Soferim* 1.8) suggest that deliberate changes to the Torah were made at the time of the translation to avoid creating misunderstanding or giving offence to Ptolemy. The persistence of these traditions may reflect ancient memories of coercion by the early Ptolemaic authorities in their efforts to promote Jewish integration into Greek society, though it is more likely that opposition to the LXX came later, and from within Judaism itself (see Fernández Marcos 2000: 44–7, and further in Chapter 4, pp. 73–5). The defensive implications of the prologue to Sirach 15–26, of Philo's remarks in *De Vita Mosis* 2.36, and of the translators' declaration of innocence in *Ep. Arist.* 306 (cf. 312–16) may point to opposition within Judaism at a later date.

The suggestion that a Greek version of the Pentateuch was needed by the Ptolemaic administration supposes that the Law of Moses functioned as the ordinary law (*politicos nomos*) of the official Jewish communities (*politeumata*) in Egypt. Parallels are drawn with translations of local Egyptian laws, for which there is documentary evidence. The theory is attractive, but founders on the nature of the Pentateuch itself which is only sporadically a law-code, and then in a very incomplete and unsystematic way (it has much to say about slavery, for instance, but very little about marriage, divorce or adoption). There may well have been a great deal of oral legislation (*halakah*) in operation but, by definition, this was not a written code. So far, also, there is no incontrovertible evidence from official Ptolemaic sources that the Pentateuch served this purpose. This is an argument from silence, but, had the Pentateuch had an official status, it is surprising that no Jewish writer mentioned it. Dorival, who is sympathetic to the proposal, finally judges that there is insufficient evidence to clinch it. We may add the consideration that, in the Hellenistic Jewish writers, 'the law' is not described in juridical terms, but presented as a source of wisdom and philosophy promoting a moral and ethical life (see, for instance, Aristobulus, Fragment 4.8 in Yarbro Collins 1985: 841).

(2) A Jewish initiative. The majority of scholars part company with *Ep. Arist.* and relate the beginnings of the LXX to new needs within the Greek-speaking Jewish communities of Egypt, especially Alexandria.

But what was the primary stimulus? Were translations needed for prayer and worship? Or for study and instruction? Or for a combination of the two? The last possibility is the most likely, as it is a mistake to treat 'liturgical' and 'educational' activities as mutually exclusive. A distinctive institution in Egyptian Jewish life was the *proseuchē*, or '[place of] prayer'. The term occurs in Egyptian inscriptions and papyri from the third century BCE onwards. The *proseuchē* was the prototype of the synagogue and seems to have been a distinctively Egyptian–Jewish development. It is likely to have provided a venue both for non-sacrificial worship and for study (Griffiths 1987: 5–6), though the earliest explicit descriptions come only in Philo and Josephus. Peters (1992: 1096) and Gruen (1998: 210), among others, take a mixed use for granted.

Some have suggested that the stimulus for translation was the need for propaganda to convince non-Jewish acquaintances of the nobility of Jewish religion and culture (e.g. Rösel 1998: 63, concerning LXX Genesis), or the need for texts when instructing Greek proselytes. Few scholars consider these factors to have been the primary *raison d'être* (Rösel is an exception), but several think they may have provided an additional motivation (see Harl, Dorival and Munnich 1988: 70, 78. Peters 1992: 1097 gives examples).

The question of Palestinian influence

Some think that the initiative came not from Egyptian Jews but from the Jerusalem high-priestly leadership or, at least, that the project was closely monitored by it (cf. *Ep. Arist.*). The presumed concern was that any Greek version should reflect reliable, authoritative Hebrew originals, perhaps with the

direct help of scholar-priests from Jerusalem. The underlying
assumption is that there was a recognized, centralized
organization, with the diaspora groups directly under the
authority of the high priest. That there were close connections
between Egypt and Palestine during the Ptolemaic period is
certain, but there is scant evidence for so tight a control by
Jerusalem in religious matters in the third century BCE
(though the so-called 'festal letters' at the beginning of 2
Maccabees (1.1–2.18), whether authentic or not, are taken to
show the official attitude of Jerusalem). It was during the
second century BCE, according to the current evidence, that
concerns about the authenticity of translations from Hebrew
began to emerge. Before that, it seems more likely that the
translation of the Pentateuch was a local initiative to meet a
variety of local needs. I will return to these questions, and
especially to the liturgical/educational debate, after considering the original translation of books other than the Pentateuch.

The translation of the Prophets and the Writings

Dating

There are no stories about the translation of these books to
help or hinder understanding, so dating is perforce from
internal evidence. This is difficult to evaluate because scholars
have been working piecemeal on the different texts, using a
variety of criteria and methodologies and sometimes producing mutually incompatible results. The summary sketched out
in 1988 by Dorival, which has been gratefully used ever since,
in fact needs careful checking (e.g. an upper limit in the third
century BCE for Psalms, Ezekiel and Minor Prophets is
questionable; see Harl, Dorival and Munnich 1988: 96–8,
111). Clarifying this rather chaotic situation and establishing
agreed criteria for dating is an urgent task.

1. *The historical books.* The translations of Joshua, Judges, 1–
   4 Kingdoms and 1–2 Paraleipomenōn tend to be placed
   in the second century BCE, somewhat earlier than 2
   Esdras and the apocryphal works. Ruth is usually dated to
   the early-first century CE (see above, Chapter 1, p. 17).

The colophon to LXX Esther yields a date before which the translation must have been made, as the book claims to have been brought to Egypt in 'the fourth year of Ptolemy and Cleopatra' (11.1); this could be either 114, or 78–77, or 48 BCE, depending on which reign is intended; there are, however, some doubts as to the authenticity of the colophon (see Reinhartz 2001: 643).

2. *The prophetic books.* For the moment, these are mostly assigned to the mid-second century BCE and later, largely from their supposed reflection of, and, in some cases, allusions to, contemporary events (Maccabean, Hasmonean, Roman, etc.). Relative connections are tentatively established by these references, where they are secure, and by attempts to establish dependence of one book on another. Daniel must be later than its Hebrew original, so dates from the mid-second century BCE at the earliest.

3. *The sapiential books.* Psalms tend to be dated somewhere in the second century BCE, though some scholars have assigned this book to the late-third century BCE, and others to the first. Proverbs and Job are usually placed in the latter half of the second century BCE. Sirach can be dated fairly precisely from the translator's prologue to between 132 and 116; scholars are divided between an earlier and a later dating. The Wisdom of Solomon and the Psalms of Solomon are usually assigned to the late-first century BCE and so, for different reasons, is the Song of Songs. Ecclesiastes may be even later (see above, Chapter 1, p. 20).

Nearly all these attempts at dating are very tentative and there is seldom a consensus.

Location

There is more debate than for the Pentateuch as to whether an Egyptian or a Palestinian background is indicated. The translation of LXX Psalms, for instance, has been variously set in both areas. The colophon to Esther suggests a Palestinian origin, the prologue to Sirach an Egyptian one.

LXX Isaiah is thought to provide internal evidence for an Egyptian setting. Words like 'private' or 'local' are sometimes used for these translations, over against 'public', 'official' or 'authoritative' for the Pentateuch. All these labels need careful examination. A theory, associated particularly with F. M. Cross, that the translations (including the Pentateuch) reflect different 'local' forms of the Hebrew text (Egyptian, Palestinian and Babylonian), has been criticized by Tov and others (see 'Further reading').

Purpose
There is no clear-cut picture. The claim that there was a Ptolemaic initiative naturally disappears, although the Ptolemies remained at least nominally in power until 30 BCE. The main area of interest – when the question is asked at all – is whether liturgical and/or educational purposes predominated, as for the Pentateuch.

The Septuagint as a whole: theories and questions

Although the translations probably played a part in both liturgical and educational life, it is helpful to look at each aspect in turn, in order to address some important issues.

The 'texts for worship' hypothesis

For those who consider liturgical factors to have been determinative, the setting for the first translations is taken to be worship in the *proseuchē*. Central to this, it is argued, would have been readings from, and exposition of, the Torah. By now the books attributed to Moses were established as the source and arbiter of law (*halakah*) and contained the community's foundational narratives (*haggadah*). Greek versions of these books were therefore needed alongside, or instead of, the Hebrew ones. The exact nature of third-century BCE diaspora liturgy is, however, controversial. Thackeray (1923) envisaged the need for a liturgical cycle of lectionary readings as the first impetus for translation. But it is unclear whether at this time the entire Torah was read in a liturgical cycle. Nor is it known when the reading of passages from the prophetic books (*haftarot*) to complement the Torah readings began, or what part was played by the Psalms. Perrot has argued strongly that there is no evidence for Pentateuchal lectionary arrangements in the third century BCE or for *haftarot* even as late as the first century CE (Harl, Dorival and Munnich 1988: 68–9).

Theories about the translation of the Pentateuch are affected by these uncertainties. If, for instance, only selections from the Torah were read at first, why would the whole Pentateuch have been translated, presumably at considerable expense (cf. Bickerman 1959: 7–8)? A further puzzle is that the Psalms, surely prime candidates for vernacular rendering, seem more likely to have been translated in the second century BCE than in the third.

Even if Thackeray's influential 'lectionary theory' is now seen to be on less firm ground, his assumption that rabbinic evidence from the second century CE, and later, could be retrojected into the third and early-second centuries BCE still colours a number of reconstructions. Earlier evidence from Philo is read back in a similarly questionable way. On other grounds, however, many scholars think it plausible that the Pentateuch at least was translated for use in public worship (e.g. Tov 1988: 168; Peters 1992: 1097; Grabbe 1992a: 200). Debates do not only concentrate on the early situation in Egypt: Schaper, for instance, argues that the Psalms were translated in Hasmonean Palestine to supply the needs of Greek-speakers in non-Temple services there (1995: 131–3, 175), though other scholars dispute this conclusion.

The question of liturgical features

If the primary motivation was liturgical, why do the translations not show more obvious marks of an adaptation to public worship? Perhaps we should ask what in fact is meant by 'liturgical': what features are we looking for in the Greek text, as distinct from the Hebrew, that would enable us to point to the *proseuchē* service as the clear *Sitz im Leben*? We might, for instance, look for more examples in the LXX than in the MT of direct address to the deity. Or for a greater use of divine titles. Or for signs of the division of the Pentateuch into the sections (*parashot* and *sedarim*) found in later Hebrew manuscripts (cf. Harl 1986: 34–43, who thinks, controversially, that LXX Genesis can be divided in this way). But even supposing that the Hebrew scrolls used by the translators were already adapted to liturgical use, how would the specific needs of a worship setting where Greek was the main language appear in translations?

LXX Psalms seem at first sight to provide some evidence: there are several superscriptions not found in the MT which apparently point to liturgical use (e.g. Ps. 23(24), 47(48), 92(93)) and may reflect Second Temple practices of using particular psalms for specific days of the week (Dorival 1999: 165–8); not all scholars, however, accept that these titles belong to the original translations (e.g. Pietersma 2000a: 29–30). The evidence needs careful weighing. In the first place, the LXX may reproduce elements already present in the Hebrew text used by the translators (there is no way of being sure of this). Secondly, superscriptions of a cultic nature are greatly outnumbered by others, also missing from the MT, of a historicizing or exegetical kind (e.g. Ps. 26(27), 64(65), 70(71), 95(96), 142(143), 145(146)), and this suggests a different emphasis overall. In any case, interest in cultic matters does not necessarily mean a cultic *Sitz im Leben*; it could equally well point to an exegetical interest in summing up the relevance of a particular psalm (cf. Pietersma 2001a: 137).

In the prophetic books, we would need, for instance, to establish whether there was more doxological material than we find in Hebrew. We might compare the final words of Amos 9.15 with the MT's direct address, where 'says the Lord *your* God' (emphasis added) perhaps suggests something more liturgical than the LXX's 'says the Lord God, the Almighty'. On the other hand, 'your' in the MT is second person singular, which could point to individual devotional reading; either way, the LXX does not suggest a liturgical emphasis. A systematic examination is, however, needed for the whole of the Minor Prophets before any conclusions can be drawn. In addition, this kind of comparison has to be handled with caution, as the indisputable later use of texts in both Jewish and Christian worship may have affected the manuscript traditions; it is often difficult to be sure whether occurrences of divine titles and so on reflect the original translation.

The question of the 'prophetic gap'

If liturgical needs prompted the translation of the Pentateuch, but the use of *haftarot* was considerably later, we might have an explanation as to why there is, apparently, a gap of one hundred years, perhaps even more, before the prophetic books were translated. Why was there such a long time-lapse? Or, to put it another way, what suddenly stimulated interest in these books around the mid-second century BCE? An answer may lie in the very different historical situation. The third century had been a relatively stable time, but the second century was marked by power struggles between Ptolemies and Seleucids and, for Jews, by the Maccabean Revolt and its consequences. It was a time of turmoil, uncertainty and conflicting loyalties, both within and without Judaism (cf. Wevers 1988: 29). Perhaps a need was felt for the old prophets to speak to a new generation, and this led to their rediscovery, their updating and, in Greek-speaking Judaism, their translation. Perhaps the prophetic message had not seemed so pressing in the third century. This is speculative, but the time-lapse requires explanation. It is not often seen as a problem by modern scholars, though Dorival uses a second-century dating of the LXX versions of the prophetic books as proof that the reading of *haftarot* was not a feature of third-century worship (Harl, Dorival and Munnich 1988: 69; cf. 110). It may be, of course, that the second-century dating of the prophetic books is wrong. Or perhaps we have, after all, overestimated the antiquity of LXX Pentateuch. In this regard, it will be helpful to consider the contribution of lexical factors to the establishment of dates.

Lexical indications of dating

Lee's important study of some Pentateuchal vocabulary (Lee 1983) establishes a range of nearly one hundred and fifty years within which to situate the Pentateuch's Greek usage (from early-third century BCE to not later than mid-second). Lee accepts as credible the 'traditional' third-century dating, relying, presumably, on the evidence of *Ep. Arist.* Evans's book on Pentateuchal verbal syntax confirms the possibility – even the probability – of an early-third-century dating 'consistent with the consensus view of c.280–250' (2001: 263). But Evans, like Lee, admits that the phenomena he analyses continue into the second century. It would be very helpful if changes in Koine Greek, whether lexical or syntactical, could be more precisely dated, so as to show when later features become apparent, and in which books or translators. This does not seem feasible until more work has been done, especially on the vocabulary of the Greek papyri (cf. Lee 2003). For the moment, on lexical-syntactical criteria alone, the translation of the Pentateuch could have occurred as late as the early-second century. Without *Ep. Arist.* we would not, perhaps, be arguing quite so confidently for a third-century date.

The 'texts for study' hypothesis

This approach locates the 'school' as the primary *Sitz im Leben.* It is taken for granted that there were Jewish schools in the third century BCE, and this seems reasonable, but there is little explicit evidence. The earliest direct reference may come in Sirach 51.23. If 'house of instruction' (*oikos paideias*; cf. Hebrew *beth midrash*) refers to an institution here, the hypothesis is less problematic for books written or translated in the second century BCE. For the third century, it is assumed that the growing Greek-speaking Jewish communities, increasingly ignorant of Hebrew, needed educating in their own traditions and sacred literature. Orlinsky, for instance, emphasizes a need for Greek-speaking Jews to be trained in the exposition of the law (1989: 536). But this scenario supposes a later, rabbinic-style approach and organization for which there is little clear evidence in third-century BCE Egypt.

If the 'school' is posited as the determining background, the same kind of question can be asked as for the liturgical hypothesis: what would we need to find in the Greek translations, as distinct from the Hebrew texts, as proof of this particular stamp? There are indeed places where, especially in the prophetic books, the LXX seems to emphasize the importance of instruction (*paideia*, often with overtones of 'discipline'). Examples can be found in Amos 3.7, Hab. 1.12, Isa. 50.4–5, Ezek. 13.9 (and cf. Bons, Joosten and Kessler 2002: 29–30 for Hosea). Again, a systematic investigation is needed before general conclusions can be drawn. In the second century BCE, as we saw in Chapter 2, *Ep. Arist.* emphasized instruction as the purpose of the law (15, 127–71, above, pp. 31–2; cf. Prov. 25.1; it is also an important theme in Philo).

The 'interlinear' model

Some scholars have argued that at least the more literal translations, including the Pentateuch and the Psalms, were originally intended as 'interlinear' aids to understanding the foundational Hebrew text. The translators, it is claimed, provided word-for-word equivalents wherever possible, paraphrased difficult or obscure passages, and added explanations ('glosses') where elements in the Hebrew risked misinterpretation. The assumption behind this theory is that the Greek versions were designed to be read alongside the Hebrew texts, to which they remained subordinate. The latter were the real objects of study, even though the Hebrew language was by now imperfectly understood. Only later, as knowledge of Hebrew diminished still further, were the Greek texts used on their own.

Proponents of this hypothesis include influential scholars like Pietersma and Wright, the co-chairs of the 'New English Translation of the Septuagint (NETS)' project (see also Chapters 6, pp. 116–17 and 7, pp. 152–4). They stress that 'interlinearity' is a metaphor, only approximately helpful and not to be pressed (cf. Hiebert 2000: 88, who allows for 'cultural updatings' in e.g. Gen. 24.22 ('earrings' for 'nose rings'); 37.28 (the price of a slave)). The disclaimer, though all too often ignored, is important: it is obvious, from the description given in the previous paragraph, that the term goes beyond what today would be expected of an interlinear 'crib'.

The hypothesis is useful in that it accounts for some of the puzzling inconsistencies in translational practice within texts. By allowing for a period of relative bilingualism (i.e. the ability to function in two languages, here both Hebrew and Greek), it also fills a logical gap between a time when all literate Jews could read the Scriptures in Hebrew and one when none, except for a few experts, had any competence at all.

But there are difficulties with the hypothesis and, as it is likely to be influential, these must be addressed. In the first place, the model rests partly on an analogy with theories about the purpose and use of Aquila's version in the early-second century CE (Brock 1972: 31; cf. Fernández Marcos 2000: 110; see further in Chapter 5, pp. 87–9). Claims for the primacy of Hebrew in the study of the Scriptures were more obviously an issue at this time, and an at least partially bilingual readership would have needed help in accessing Hebrew texts. But this kind of situation cannot be retrojected into the third and second centuries BCE without good evidence to support it. Such evidence is largely lacking: we do not know enough about the circumstances of bilingualism then, or about attitudes towards the relative importance of Hebrew and Greek as vehicles for the study of Scripture (or how Aramaic fits into the picture). Another questionable assumption is that the Hebrew text used by the translators was essentially the same as the MT.

Boyd-Taylor (1998) sharpens the focus with the use of the term 'metaphrase' (i.e. word-for-word translation, or close paraphrase). The verb *metaphrazō* is found in Greek writers and in Josephus (e.g. *Antiquities of the Jews* (*Ant.*) 8.144). Boyd-Taylor applies it to the way the text of Homer is handled in some Egyptian school-papyri. These contain both word-for-word renderings of straightforward verses (from Homeric into Koine Greek) and paraphrases of difficult passages. This leads him to set the origins of the LXX in the context of Jewish attempts to create their own literate tradition. He posits the growth of Jewish schools in the Greek style and emphasizes the need for the Greek-speaking community to have access to its foundational texts in the original language (Boyd-Taylor 1998: 73–6). This has the advantage of using a model from the right period, though the analogy is not quite exact, as the Homeric 'metaphrases' operate within the same language. But it is still assumed that the Greek translations were intended only to provide access to the Hebrew, and this is not certain (the later Latin-Greek Virgil 'cribs', noted by Brock 1972: 29–31, provide more interesting comparisons for Aquila than for the earlier period).

There is a marked difference between the 'interlinear' or 'metaphrase' approaches and the more usual view that the LXX was intended to be used independently of the Hebrew texts from the start (e.g. Bogaert 1985: 197; Fernández Marcos 2001: 235). The fundamental question is the status of the Hebrew text. It is clear that by the time of Philo it was necessary to defend the equality of the Greek text with the Hebrew (hence his insistence on the LXX as miraculous and inspired; see Chapter 4, pp. 64–70), and LXX fragments from the second and first centuries BCE already show signs of 'correction' against a proto-Masoretic text-form. But how far back can we find a demonstrable difference in status between the two vehicles of sacred tradition? The relatively stable third century BCE does not provide evidence that Hebrew and Greek versions of Scripture were seen as rivals, or that the Hebrew must continue to be read at all costs.

The question of style

One feature which is not sufficiently accounted for in the 'interlinear' or 'metaphrase' hypotheses is the appearance in the LXX of stylistic features which often create new literary patterns and resonances, not strictly needed for the elucidation of the Hebrew. Austermann has addressed this phenomenon in LXX Psalms (in a paper given during the eleventh Congress of the IOSCS at Basel in August 2001, publication forthcoming; cf. Austermann 2000: 382). He argues, against the 'interlinear' approach, that it points to the conscious creation of a new kind of literature (though, like Schaper, he posits a cultic rather than an educational *Sitz im Leben*). Evans, too, comments on the presence of many 'stylistic flourishes' in the Pentateuch (2001: 263). Some examples will illustrate the point.

(1) Amos 1.3–2.6. Throughout the book, the translator renders his Hebrew meticulously, at the same time coping in various ways with difficulties as he encounters them (Dines 1992). In many ways he fits the 'interlinear' bill. In 1.3–2.6, however, his handling of the 'Oracles against the Nations' provides an interesting additional feature of his technique.

In the MT, this lengthy passage contains formulaic introductions and statements of crimes committed by different nations. The only variations are the suffixes in 1.11 and 2.1, but these may be intended to create a slightly uneven chiasm, with 1.13 at the centre. The LXX has some surprising differences. The essential elements are as follows:

	LXX	MT
1.3	**anth'hōn** *eprizon*	*'al-dûšām*
	(**since** they sawed)	(because they threshed)
1.6	*heneken* tou *aichmalōteusai*	*'al-haglôtām*
	(*on account of* capturing)	(because they exiled)
1.9	**anth'hōn** *sunekleisan*	*'al-hasgîrām*
	(**since** they hemmed in)	(because they delivered up)
1.11	*heneka* tou *diōxai*	*'al-rod^{e}pô*
	(*on account of* pursuing)	(because he pursued)
1.13	**anth'hōn** *aneschizon*	*'al-biq'ām*
	(**since** they ripped up)	(because they cut open)
2.1	**anth'hōn** *katekausan*	*' al-sor^{e}pô*
	(**since** they burned)	(because he burned)
2.4	*heneka* tou *apōsasthai*	*'al-mo'^{o}sām*
	(*on account of* rejecting)	(because they rejected)
2.6	**anth'hōn** *apedonto*	*'al-mikrām*
	(**since** they sold)	(because they sold)

In each case, the MT has *'al* with infinitive construct and suffix to express the nature of the crime ('because they/he . . . '). But the LXX has a regular alternation between *anth'hōn* with imperfect or aorist (which also alternate) and *heneken* (or *heneka*) with articular aorist infinitive; both give the same sense. The break in sequence between 1.13 and 2.1 (*anth'hōn* twice) ensures a final *anth'hōn* in 2.6, so creating an *inclusio* with 1.3, which the strict sequence would have lost (the chiastic pattern also matches 1.11–2.1 in the MT).

What is this sophisticated rendering for? It serves no grammatical, syntactic or exegetical purpose; it is not a help (rather the opposite) to showing 'how the Hebrew works', which is supposedly the 'interlinear' aim, and there is no question here of a different source-text (*Vorlage*). It is surely intended to make a rather lengthy and cumbersome passage more interesting (cf. Muraoka 2002b: xix). And this suggests that the aesthetic sense of a Greek readership is being addressed in the study of a Greek text.

There is nothing else as arresting in LXX Amos in other sequences where one might have expected it (e.g. 3.3–6; 4.6–11; 7.1–6, though these are all shorter than 1.3–2.6). Amos 9.2–4 does have an alternation, not found in the MT, between *ean*, 'if' (2a, 3a), and *kai ean*, 'and if' (2b, 3b), while in 9.11 there is a striking stylistic difference between the LXX and the MT. Here, the LXX has two pairs of matching verbs (first and third, and second and fourth), whereas the MT has only one (first and third). In addition, all four verbs in the LXX begin with *ana-*. The following table shows the differences:

LXX	MT
*ana*stēso (*I will raise* **up**) *ano*ikodomēso (*I will build* **up**)	'āqîm (*I will raise*)
	(wᵉ)gādartî (… *I will wall in*)
*ana*stēso (*I will raise* **up**) *ano*ikodomēso (*I will build* **up**)	'āqîm (*I will raise*)
	(û)bᵉnîtî(hā) (… *I will build…*)

Muraoka draws attention to a similar literary effect in Jer. 2.6, where there are four adjectives beginning with *a-* (1973: 24–6). He also notes another example of alternation in Hag. 1.5, 7; 2.15, 18 (*taxate/thesthe* for Hebrew *sîmû*, 2002b: xix–xx). Harl notes a possible example in Zeph. 3.8 (1999: 187–9). Lee makes the apposite observation that 'elegant variation' is a standard stylistic device in Hellenistic Greek rhetoric and the one, in fact, most evident in the LXX (1997: 776–8; he illustrates, from Ps. 3, other stylistic 'borrowings'; 1997: 781–2).

2. Gen. 1.2. Proof that this stylistic awareness is not a feature of the second generation of translators, as it were, but occurs from the start, can be seen in Gen. 1.2, where there is an apparently careful choice of words beginning with *a-* and ending in *-os*, including a coinage, *abussos* (in its grammatically required genitive form, *abussou*):

LXX	*Hē de gē ēn **a**horat**os** kai **a**kataskeuast**os** kai skotos epanō tēs **a**buss**ou*** (The earth, however, was **un**seen and **un**sorted and darkness [was] over the **un**sounded [depth])
MT	*Wᵉhā'āreṣ hayᵉtâ **tōhû wābōhû** wᵉḥōšek 'al-pᵉnê **tᵉhôm*** (But the earth was **a vast waste** (REB) and [there was] darkness upon the **deep**)

Perhaps the translator is trying to echo the sound pattern of *tōhû, bōhû* and *tᵉhôm* in a different way with *a*horat*os*, *a*kataskeuast*os* and *a*buss*ou* (cf. Dines 1995: 444–5), but he seems to go beyond the bounds of interlinear duty.

These are only a few examples, though they are telling ones. If this aesthetic quality turns out to be a widespread phenomenon, it will make it unlikely that the translations were intended only to give access to the Hebrew text. (At the other extreme, Rösel has suggested that Genesis was translated 'as an original Jewish-Hellenistic contribution to the discussions of the *museion* or the famous *library* in Alexandria', 1998: 63; original emphasis.) Clearly, much more work needs to be done in this area where scholars are coming to opposite conclusions about the same translations. The evidence so far suggests that an initial stage of very close rendering of Hebrew texts, perhaps even oral, may well have existed and have left its mark on the LXX, but that most of the translations as we now have them witness to a more consciously literary development (cf. Harl 2001: 185).

The question of official translations

There is one further question concerning LXX origins arising from the 'interlinear' theory: was there, from the beginning, only one 'authorized' translation for each book? The question is prompted by the puzzle of the non-homogeneity of the LXX where translations vary greatly in their degree of 'literalness' or 'freedom'. The 'interlinear' theory only works for 'literal' translations which reproduce their source-text closely; it does not pretend to cover the 'free' translations such as Job, Proverbs or Daniel. But both types need to be accounted for. Why did some translators translate 'literally' and others 'freely'? And how did both types come to be included in the traditional LXX? If, as is often claimed, the translations were officially commissioned and carefully supervised, why were such different styles of translation permitted? Some scholars distinguish between the Pentateuch, whose special status meant that the translators kept close to the Hebrew, and the other books which were more 'private' or 'informal' translations and where the translators sat more lightly to their source-texts. But examples of 'free' translation occur in the Pentateuch, especially in Exodus, while some of the later books are extremely literal; in any case, the distinction does not explain how all the disparate texts came together. Tov imagines a haphazard assembling of scrolls – editors using whatever they could find – and comments on the apparent lack of collaboration between translators (1997: 15). This might suggest that there were alternative versions circulating simultaneously (a more 'literal' translation of Isaiah, for instance) which just did not happen to be available at the crucial moment and were soon lost.

   The question is important because there has been a controversy as to whether there were multiple translations of LXX books or only one translation for each book. The controversy goes back to two great scholars: Paul de Lagarde and Paul Kahle (see Jobes and Silva 2000: 242–5, 274–6). Each studied the textual complexity of the LXX manuscripts, and came to a radically different conclusion. Lagarde believed that it was possible to tease out the original form of each translation, and that there had, in fact, been only one translation (an *Urtext*) for each book. Kahle examined the same evidence and concluded that the text of the LXX had emerged gradually from an initial plurality of versions more akin to the Aramaic Targums; official selection had come only late and as a Christian initiative, after which alternative versions stopped circulating. Subsequent events, especially the progressive discovery of the Dead Sea Scrolls, have led to an almost universal acceptance of Lagarde's position, which now undergirds most textual work on the LXX, especially that of Göttingen (see above, Chapter 1, p. 9). Kahle's position has been largely rejected. More recently, however, work on the double texts (Tobit, Daniel, etc.; see above, Chapter 1, pp. 18, 23) and on the early revisions has shown that the division between original translation and recensional development is not so clear-cut (cf. Tov 1997: 11; Wevers 1999: 461). Available manuscript evidence points to a single archetype (a text, or presumed text, from which all members of a manuscript 'family' are descended) for most, but not quite all, books. The claim of the Göttingen editors to be able to recover these archetypes is generally well founded. Ulrich (2000), however, doubts whether LXX Psalms really preserves the original translation and Jellicoe comments that the faulty archetype of Sir. 32–6 (above, Chapter 1, p. 21) is unlikely to represent the original translation (1968: 307). The question remains as to why the archetypes are of such different kinds. Although lip-service is paid to the fact that archetype does not necessarily mean autograph (the presumed original translation itself; Tov 1988: 165 remarks on Lagarde's blurring of this distinction), that is what we all assume in practice, jumping what could be called 'the Göttingen gap'.

If the *Urtext* theory is to work, some kind of organization and control at the time the translations were made seems necessary, and the relative uniformity of the majority of books, with their broadly literal style, does seem to support this. Perhaps, after all, Kahle was right to think in terms of a deliberate selection of texts which then led to the disappearance of other candidates. Only this seems likely to have started much earlier than he thought, perhaps in the mid-second century BCE. But, once again, why were the 'free' translations

included? Perhaps, as Tov suggested, it was simply a question
of 'the luck of the draw', of the circulation, survival and
availability of scrolls. If so, the official supervision assumed to
have been exercised by Jerusalem, was less firm than usually
depicted. The likelihood of this kind of control over diaspora
communities has already been questioned (above, pp. 43, 44–
5, 58). A simpler explanation may be that there were not very
many people sufficiently expert to do the work of translation, a
time-consuming and costly affair. Perhaps, too, the variety in
style of translation is no more surprising than the variety found
within the Hebrew Bible itself. All the same, the 'one book,
one translation' theory, although tidy (and attractive perhaps
for those concerned with Scripture as authoritative), is really
rather extraordinary. The textual evidence is already being
reassessed (see the quotations from Fernández Marcos in
Jobes and Silva 2000: 276); there will be repercussions for
theories of LXX origins that are likely to be of considerable
importance.

The question of the Septuagint

This brings us back, finally, to the fundamental question: why
were written Scriptures needed, or permitted, in Greek at a
time when they were not, apparently, in Aramaic? Why could
there not have been oral Greek paraphrases of the Hebrew
Scriptures in Egypt which might eventually have resulted in
written Greek 'Targums'? The usual explanations, as we have
seen, relate to the internal needs of Greek-speaking Jews. But
there may have been other stimuli as well. Alexandria
(assuming the whole enterprise to have started there)
provided a literate, cosmopolitan culture, where 'everyone
who was anyone' came to study, and where debating and
writing were second nature. Alexandrian Judaism may have
almost accidentally pioneered a new stage in the history of the
Bible in response to the excitement of living in an educated
milieu which expressed itself in written words (cf. Lee 1997:
776 for the translators' educational level). Books were
produced, not exactly because they were needed, but because
this was the natural thing to do. Perhaps this helps to explain

the translators' occasional delight in finding stylish equivalents for Hebrew effects, or in creating new stylistic effects (Gen. 1.2, Amos 1.3–2.6, and elsewhere). It is true that this would be more likely to result in new works written by Jews in Greek, and there is a rich repertoire of such works, both from Egypt and from Palestine (see Chapter 7, pp. 136–8). But we may speculate that the intellectual impetus also led to the almost revolutionary idea of making translations. This was a moment of creative genius from which the LXX emerged as something generically new: not quite like a legislative document, not quite like a metaphrase of Homer, not quite an exegetical rewriting, but exhibiting features of all these genres. The first translators made serious use of all of them as appropriate ways of rendering the holy books in use within their communities, and in doing so perhaps attracted the interest of the wider world as well.

Further reading

The introductions listed at the end of Chapter 1 all deal with questions of dating, location and purpose. For two valiant, but questionable, attempts to pinpoint the year of the translation of the Pentateuch, contrast Collins (1992 [281 BCE]) and Rösel (1994: 66 [c. 247 BCE]). For evaluations of Cross's 'local texts' theory, see Harl, Dorival and Munnich (1988: 186–7, 190–2); Tov (1997: 185–7).

For evidence of diaspora Jewish settlements throughout the Hellenistic world, see Schürer (1986: 3–86); Barclay (1996). The history of the Jewish communities in Ptolemaic Egypt, and their status, is complex and controversial. The contrasting analyses of Hegermann (1989: 115–66) and Gruen (1998: 199, 203, 222–30, 240–5) cover much of the ground. See also Swete (1914: 4–8); Bartlett (1985: 1–10); Harl, Dorival and Munnich (1988: 31–8). For relations between Egyptian and Palestinian Jews, see Kasher (1991).

On the *proseuchē* and the early development of the synagogue, see Griffiths (1987); Hegermann (1989: 151–4); Reif (1993: 71–87).

On the 'interlinear' hypothesis, see Pietersma (2000a; 2001b). More details on the NETS project will be found at the end of Chapter 7, p. 153.

For a discussion of the implications of bilingualism, see Fernández Marcos (2000: 9–12).

CHAPTER 4

The Status of the Septuagint: from Philo to Jerome

Introduction

Whatever the historical circumstances behind it, *Ep. Arist.* established a story of beginnings which entered the Jewish and Christian imagination and led to developments both hagiographical and ideological.

Ep. Arist. does not describe the translation as miraculous, merely observing that its completion by the seventy-two translators in seventy-two days was somehow providential (307). The consensus method used, whereby each section was debated until all agreed (302), resembles standard practices in Alexandrian scholarship. The many improbabilities in the story, not least the vast number of translators in the first place, do, however, create a sense of the marvellous which later writers develop.

The subsequent stress on miraculous elements is important because it reveals something about the controversies that arose concerning the relative merits of the Hebrew and Greek versions or, more precisely, about whether the LXX was authoritative in the same way as was apparently being claimed for the Hebrew scrolls.

Hints of this challenge, discernible already in the fragmentary remains of the LXX dating from the second century BCE, first become explicit in Philo and are a key to understanding how this great Jewish scholar, exegete, philosopher and statesman views the LXX.

63

Philo of Alexandria (*c.* 20 BCE – *c.* 50 CE)

Philo on the making of the Septuagint

Philo speaks about the LXX in Book 2 of his *Life of Moses* (*De Vita Mosis* 2.25–44). In Book 1 he has dealt with the events of Moses' life. Now, in Book 2, he discusses Moses' character as exemplifying the virtues of philosopher-king, lawgiver, high priest and prophet. As king and lawgiver (the two cannot be separated), Moses' excellence is demonstrated chiefly in the character of the laws that he wrote 'under God's guidance' in 'the sacred books', and which have remained unchanged ever since (this suggests that he acknowledges the authority of the Hebrew text) so that even pagans recognize and honour the Jewish law. The account of the translating of the law on Philadelphus's initiative is then given as further proof of non-Jewish appreciation.

The immediate context is the claim that 'some people, thinking it a shame that the laws should be found in one half only of the human race, the barbarians, and denied altogether to the Greeks, took steps to have them translated' (*De Vita Mosis* 2.27). Philo thus continues the trend, already found in *Ep. Arist.* and Aristobulus (above, Chapter 2) of presenting the Jewish Scriptures ('the laws') as a treasure which the Greek-speaking world, once it knew about it, was eager to share. Amir claims that, in Philo's eyes, once the law was universally available in Greek, the Hebrew original was no longer important (1988: 443). But this seems unlikely. The claim is for equality; both versions should be treated 'with awe and reverence as sisters or rather one and the same, both in matter and words' (*De Vita Mosis* 2.40). The comment by Jobes and Silva that 'Philo's ... elaborations confirm that in the Hellenistic period the Septuagint was revered by many Jews as the divinely inspired text, *perhaps* on a par with the Hebrew Scriptures' (2000: 82; emphasis added) seems unnecessarily cautious. It may be wondered, too, whether the Hebrew texts themselves were explicitly regarded as 'inspired' until the existence of the LXX forced the issue.

Borgen links Philo's approach to the LXX with his eschatology (cf. *De Vita Mosis* 2.44). The Jews, Philo claims, are destined to become world-leaders not by force (he is perhaps thinking of the failed Jewish uprising following the death of Caligula in 41 CE, though he does not say so), but by their God-given laws – and the prosperity gained through keeping them – which will lead to universal conversion. 'Philo's writings', Borgen says, 'serve the general aim of interpreting these laws to the surrounding world and preparing the Jews for their universal task' (1992: 336–7).

Because the project was so momentous, no one less than Philadelphus, 'the most famous of kings', could be approached. Philo's eulogy of Philadelphus (*De Vita Mosis* 2.29–30) includes the claim that the king's munificence has become so proverbial that any particularly lavish gifts or grand building projects are called 'Philadelphian' (*philadelphaious*). Perhaps it was this reputation that originally led to the story of the translation being attached to him, as a *sine qua non*. The tradition of 'the translation made for King Talmai (i.e. Ptolemy)' persists in rabbinic sources too, e.g. *b. Meg.* 9a–b (Veltri 1994; see further below, pp. 73–5). So, following the story-line of *Ep. Arist.*, Philo gives the initiative to Philadelphus as the result of divine inspiration. Philadelphus consults the high priest; the high priest appoints the translators; the translators answer the king's philosophical questions (though not in such detail as in *Ep. Arist.*); the translations they produce are identical.

Special features in Philo's account

There are, however, several differences between Philo's account and that of *Ep. Arist.*

1. The number of translators is not mentioned, nor that they worked for seventy-two days.

2. The completed translation is not read to, nor approved by, the Jewish community.

3. There is no reference to Demetrius of Phalerum. This may indicate either that Philo was aware of the historical

problem, or (more probably) that Demetrius was surplus to his requirements: Philo's interest is in kingly figures, and Demetrius, although one-time tyrant of Athens, is no longer a ruler at the time of the story. Or he may have wanted to emphasize the part played by the supernatural.

4. The high priest Eleazer is called 'king'. Perhaps Philo wants to put him on the same level as Philadelphus, despite the anachronism (the Hasmonean priestly dynasty adopted the title of king only in the time of Aristobulus I, 104–103 BCE, or Alexander Jannaeus, 103–76). Or perhaps 'king and priest' go so closely together in Philo's treatment of Moses that the identification affects the notion of high priesthood as such: for Philo, Moses was necessarily king and high priest, and here the identification may be working in reverse.

5. The island, unnamed in *Ep. Arist.*, is identified as Pharos and described as 'the place in which the light of that version shone out'. Is Philo likening the LXX to Isaiah's prophecy of 'a light to the nations', cf. Isa. 49.6? Or thinking perhaps of Sir. 24.32, where wisdom/Torah will radiate instruction (*paideia*) like the dawn, 'to a great distance (*heōs eis makran*)'?

6. The translators choose where to go and are accommodated in separate houses which, he says, can still be seen. There is an annual festival, still kept in his day, to honour the site of the translation and to thank God for the completion of the 'good gift, so old, yet ever young' (*De Vita Mosis* 2.41). Greeks as well as Jews participate; Philo takes this as evidence of universal belief in the inspired nature of the LXX. There is a panegyric, a final banquet and a night spent in huts built on the island.

7. The agreement of the translators is the result not of comparison and discussion, but of divine inspiration so that, although they work separately, all come up with identical translations. This makes their work prophetic, and is itself proof of the miraculous nature of the translation.

8. Another kind of difference between the two works is that, while *Ep. Arist.* claims to be an eye-witness account, so drawing the reader into the time of the supposed events, Philo reports a past event from the point of view of his own perceptions and beliefs. This makes it easier for us to grasp what the event, and the LXX itself, signifies for Philo, whereas in the case of the pseudepigraphical *Ep. Arist.*, we have to deduce the authorial attitudes from the narrative.

Philo on the 'inspiration' of the Septuagint

To understand what Philo says, we must look more closely at his language. In *De Vita Mosis* 2.36 he describes the translators' working conditions, near the seashore, in idyllic terms. He then describes the translation-event itself:

> sitting here in seclusion, with none present save the elements of nature – earth, water, air, heaven – of whose genesis they were about to give the first sacred exposition (*hierophantēsein*) – for the laws begin with the story of the world's creation – [and] as if divinely possessed (*kathaper enthousiōntes*), they proclaimed [literally 'prophesied'] (*proephēteuon*), not some one thing and some another, but all of them identical words and phrases, as though a prompter [or 'interpreter'] (*hupoboleōs*), was calling out (*enēchountos*) to each one individually without being seen.
>
> (*De Vita Mosis* 2.37; translation adapted
> from Colson 1966: 467)

Philo's vocabulary in this passage requires more thorough treatment than can be attempted here, but some of the salient features can be indicated.

1. *hierophantēsein*. In classical Greek, the verb *hierophantein* can mean 'to be a hierophant', that is, the one who initiates people into the mystery cults (cf. Lucian, *Alexander* 39), especially the priest at Eleusis. It also carries the sense of instructing people in the mysteries, or of expounding their meaning. Herodotus uses the

term more generally of anyone who teaches rituals (*Histories* 7.153). Philo adopts the verb, and its associated noun *hierophantēs*, to describe the roles of Moses (*De virtutibus* 163, 174) and the high priest (*De specialibus legibus.* 3.135), as well as the translators (*De Vita Mosis* 2.37). The combination of religious and didactic elements made it an effective, if daring, choice. The word is used frequently by Philo, although it does not occur in the LXX.

2. *enthousiōntes.* The verb *enthousiaō* (or *enthousiazō*), 'to be possessed', is a technical term for inspiration, that is, divine possession and its manifestations. It is a term used often by Plato. In *Apology* 22C, for instance, it refers to poets who do not understand the words they have been 'given' to write. In *Phaedrus* 253A, the lover is obsessively 'possessed' by the beloved, and in 241E, the 'enthusiast' is someone being driven out of his mind! In Plato, at least, there are negative resonances to the term. It too is absent from the LXX (it may occur in Sir. 31(34).7, of inordinate desire for gold, but the reading is not certain; see Ziegler 1965: 269). Philo clearly uses the word in an entirely positive way, as he links it with 'prophesying' (for other occurrences, see Borgen 2000: 130; cf. Isaacs 1976: 48–51).

3. *proephēteuon.* Instead of saying 'they began to write', Philo says 'they prophesied', thus putting the work of translation on the same level as the original 'inspired' composition by Moses. *Proephēteuon* is also the main verb, and so the main focus, in Philo's very complex sentence.

4. *hupoboleus*, literally, 'one who suggests, or reminds', is used for the 'prompter' in a theatre (Plutarch, *Moralia* 813F; cf. 404B), and is translated as such by Colson in *De Vita Mosis* 2.37, but in Philo the term occurs also in parallel with *hermēneus*, 'interpreter' (e.g. *De migratione Abrahami* 78–80), so may have wider implications here.

5. *enēchountos. Enēcheō*, 'to resonate', denotes, in all contexts, loud or persistent noise (see e.g. Plutarch, *Moralia*

589D, of an interior 'echo'; Onosander, *The General* 1.13, of a trumpet call; Philo, *Quis rerum divinarum heres sit* 67, 71; *De mutatione nominum* 57; *De specialibus legibus* 1.65; 4.49). The verb fits well with what Philo is trying to say: Greek theatres required more than a discreet whisper from the prompter, if this is really the image suggested by *hupoboleus* (cf. Colson and Whitaker 1968: 588, who draw attention to the 'noisy' implications of *enēcheō*); the idea of the 'interpreter' is perhaps more likely to be paramount. But Philo may be thinking of both images simultaneously; the fact that the 'voice' is 'unseen' might suggest both the prompter in the wings and the heavenly provenance of the inspired words (cf. below, 2.40).

What Philo seems to be suggesting, then, in his bold use of language borrowed from Greek religious and cultural life, is that the translators responded, in a trance-like state, to an insistent voice which 'interpreted' (or 'relayed') the Hebrew for them. As prophets and hierophants they resemble Moses, whose work they continue.

When Philo speaks of 'inspiration', does he intend only the Pentateuch, or does he include the Prophets and Writings, most, if not all, of which have by now been translated? He certainly considers the two latter categories to be 'holy' and sometimes quotes from them (though not from any of the apocryphal books), but the bulk of his scriptural texts are from the Pentateuch, which he clearly regards as being in a class of its own because of its Mosaic authorship (see Amir 1988; Williamson 1989. For Philo's exegetical practice, see Chapter 7, pp. 140–1).

A defence of the Septuagint against accusations of inaccuracy?

Some of Philo's remarks suggest that he is defending the reliability of the translation, and this may point to the existence of challenges to the inerrancy of the LXX, perhaps from people making or using revised versions. This can be seen in *De Vita Mosis* 2.34–40, where the translators knew 'how great an undertaking it was to make a full version of the laws given by the Voice of God, where they could not add or take away or transfer anything but must keep the original form and shape' (34). There was no paraphrasing, he continues; the translation was completely literal, because to change the form would be to change the meaning. The proof is that those who have learned the other language (whether Greek or Hebrew) find both versions identical.

If Philo really believes this, he has not made detailed comparisons between the two versions (indeed, his knowledge of Hebrew was probably rudimentary). Or perhaps he knew – or knew of – Hebrew texts that were much closer to the presumed sources of the LXX than are now extant. In fact, his own LXX sources were not homogeneous, as the nature of his citations makes clear (although for the most part his text is close to that of Vaticanus). Where he appears to be closer to a revised text, one must suppose that he was not aware of the difference, but used whatever scrolls he had to hand, without knowing their prehistory. We might assume that this was an attitude typical of an age before the development of textual criticism, were it not that Alexandrian scholarship had already laid the foundations for such awareness. Philo's claims, set in the context of divine inspiration, have a polemic ring. The concern for accuracy does not, in any case, extend to his use of the LXX in exegesis, for here he often paraphrases and rewrites his biblical material (see Borgen 1997: 46–62). But in *De Vita Mosis* he is concerned with the initial translation, not the way in which it is subsequently used.

Philo's contribution to the story of LXX origins marks the beginning of a stress on the supernatural character of the translation. The effect is to underline the importance of the Greek version and its authenticity over against the Hebrew Bible. It is an emphasis and a *parti pris* that were to have enormous influence on Christian apologists. Set in his own historical context, Philo provides evidence of how attitudes towards the sacred texts had developed and changed since the writing of *Ep. Arist.*, a century or more earlier.

Josephus (37 – *c.* 100 CE)

Like Philo's *Life of Moses,* Josephus's *Antiquities of the Jews* (*Ant.*) was written with non-Jews in mind. In effect, it is an account of Israel's history from Genesis to the Maccabees. In Book 12.12–118, Josephus retells the story of the translating of the Pentateuch, paraphrasing and abbreviating *Ep. Arist.* for the purpose. Despite the shortening, it is a very full account, unparalleled in Josephus's use of sources in the rest of *Ant.* The space given to the story shows how important the LXX was to Josephus as a biblical source, even though, like Philo, he often paraphrases extensively or rewrites completely.

Comparison with *Ep. Arist.* shows that Josephus's alterations are often of a stylistic nature, reflecting literary fashions of the first century CE (suggesting perhaps that *Ep. Arist.* sounded old-fashioned by now). The rewriting of the LXX may have had similar motivation, and in any case it was good authorial style to disguise one's sources (cf. Spottorno 1997: 382). Given that Josephus is paraphrasing *Ep. Arist.*, it is not surprising that there are no radical differences with the original story-line. The only new factor is Josephus's reference to the seventy-two translators (he specifically mentions that there were six from each tribe) as 'the seventy' (*Ant.* 12.57). This is the earliest attestation of the title that was to become the standard way of referring not just to the translators but to the text itself. It is less likely to be a convenient round number than a deliberate evocation, alongside the significant 'six from each tribe', of biblical groups of seventy (Orlinsky 1989: 539). Obvious examples would be Exod. 24.1, 9 and Num. 11.16–17. (In reverse direction are Gen. 46.27, Exod. 1.5, where the 75 descendants of Jacob according to the LXX and to 4Q1(4QGen-Exod[a]) are given as 70 in the MT; Fernández Marcos 2000: 73).

Of greater interest is Josephus's setting for his lengthy retelling of *Ep. Arist.* It comes in his treatment of the reign of Ptolemy II Philadelphus, which means that his emphasis is on the relationship between Jews and their foreign rulers: 'These, then, were the things done by Ptolemy Philadelphus in appreciation and honour of the Jews' (*Ant.* 12.118). Josephus then demonstrates a similar success with the Seleucids of Asia. The LXX is introduced not as a subject in its own right, but as an illustration of a political attitude (cf. Aristobulus and Greek philosophy, above, Chapter 2, p. 36).

There is perhaps a hint of contemporary debate about which version should be followed. Concerning the curse with which the original translation was protected (*Ep. Arist.* 311), Josephus merely says that where alterations creep in, the text should be restored to the original. This still gives authority to the traditional version, but also demonstrates how little was known about that version, since the text used by Josephus seems to have been closer to the Antiochian type than anything (see Chapter 5, p. 104).

Continuation of the Septuagint legends in Judaism

The emphasis in our earliest sources, as we have seen, is both on the superiority of Jewish religion and culture alongside that of the Greeks (relations with the outside world), and on the equality of the LXX with the Hebrew versions in reliability and/or inspiration (relations within Judaism). As we move into the succeeding centuries, there are developments and shifts of emphasis, both within Judaism and in relation to the nascent Christian churches, which affect the status of the LXX.

After the catastrophes of 70 and 135 CE (the failed Jewish rebellions against Rome), the trend to favour one particular form of the Hebrew text of Scripture, already discernible earlier, becomes more prominent in the West. The learning of Hebrew is encouraged, and there is a concern to preserve the text of Scripture in its supposedly unique original form (however unrealistic this may have been). With only the proto-Masoretic consonantal text-type now acceptable, other strands of Hebrew tradition disappear as scrolls with variant text-types cease to be copied. Greek, however, continues to be widely used in much of the Roman Empire, so the LXX remains an important vehicle of Scripture. It is not surprising that the perpetuation, in the LXX, of what were now perceived to be inaccurate translations led to disquiet. The fact that the

LXX was being vigorously used by Christians in proselytizing and in academic Jewish-Christian debate, added to the unease of many rabbinic authorities.

The most striking development was the promotion of at least three major Jewish versions in Greek, traditionally assigned to Aquila, Symmachus and Theodotion (often referred to as 'the Three'). These will be considered in Chapter 5. Here, it is important to situate them in their historical context, which is one of movements within Judaism itself and not just of reaction to Christianity, as is often asserted. Nor should it be thought that Jews stopped using the LXX overnight, or that all reactions to it were negative. In fact, the presence of both positive and negative judgements in the few rabbinic texts which deal with the LXX is one of their most interesting features.

Rabbinic sources and the Septuagint

Positive attitudes

The main source here is the Babylonian Talmud, *Meg.* 9a–b. The remarks on the LXX come in the context of whether there is a distinction between writing in scrolls and writing in *mezuzoth* and *tefillin*; that is, the discussion is not about the LXX as such. There is a reference to the existence of the translators' separate 'rooms' on Pharos; this appears earlier in Christian writers but in Jewish sources seems to be of second-century origin (Jellicoe 1968: 43, n. 1, citing Hadas). The tradition probably derives from Philo's insistence that the translators worked separately (above, p. 66). It also occurs in the Jerusalem Talmud (*y. Meg.* 1.1, 4) in a discussion on the languages into which the law can be adequately translated: only Greek is permitted. This indicates the venerable nature of the LXX and the way in which it was, albeit grudgingly, accepted.

Also in the second century CE, according to rabbinic sources, the designation of the seventy-two translators as 'the seventy' occurs, as in Josephus. This too is shared with Christian writers. It suggests that Philo's emphasis on the inspired nature of the LXX had not entirely vanished from rabbinic perceptions (references to the separate houses may go in the same direction).

Negative attitudes

The miraculous agreement of the translators is also put to more negative use. At some point, a tradition emerged that the translators had deliberately changed certain verses in the LXX in order to avoid scandalizing King Ptolemy or creating misunderstandings of the Torah. In the Minor Tractate *b. Masseket Soferim* 1.8, the miraculous element is that 'the seventy-two' were all inspired to make the same alterations. An alternative story appears in 1.7, with only five translators, though this probably stems from a misreading (Orlinsky 1989: 538, n. 2; contra Fernández Marcos 2000: 47). The number of these alterations varies, and they do not all correspond to current forms of the LXX. They probably reflect rabbinic exegetical responses to problematic verses in the MT, rather than textual differences in the LXX resulting from a different source-text (though some, e.g. Tov, would disagree). The grounding of these passages in the historical circumstances of the first translation, however, suggests that the debates have deep roots going back to very early perceptions of differences between the Hebrew and Greek texts.

Survival of the LXX in Judaism

The debates about permitted languages, and the toleration only of Greek, have to be seen against controversies over translations into Aramaic and the writing down of Targums. This in turn points to struggles for ascendancy between different groups in Babylonian and Palestinian Judaism and the (reluctant?) recognition of the continuation of Greek as the language of many Jews. The rabbinic evidence, despite its ambivalent attitudes, shows that the LXX went on being regarded as a phenomenon quite different from other versions, and certainly on a different standing from the Targums. It was not entirely rejected or neglected by the rabbis ('LXX traditions existed alongside the Masoretic tradition for centuries', Büchner 1997: 404; cf. Harl 1992: 11–15) and its problematic position was only partly affected by Christianity. Veltri claims that the strongly negative attitude arises only in the Gaonic period (seventh century CE onwards), with the belief that a fully satisfactory translation of the Torah was an impossibility (1994: 22–112; summary in Fernández Marcos 2000: 47, n. 54; 'by King Ptolemy' here should be 'for King Ptolemy'). The proof that an acceptance of texts in Greek continued into medieval Judaism is demonstrated by the fact that new versions continued to be made even after 'the Three'. These sometimes show signs of contact with the LXX for, despite the renaissance of Hebrew as the language of Judaism *par excellence*, the truth is that there were still many Greek-speaking Jews in the Byzantine Empire, hidden heirs to 'the brilliant culture of Hellenistic Judaism' (Fernández Marcos 2000: 185; cf. Harl 1986: 10).

Continuation of the Septuagint legends in Christianity

Because Christianity originated mainly within Greek-speaking Judaism, Christians naturally used the Greek versions of Scripture. At first, as the NT shows, this was done without comment or apology. But during the second century CE, controversies with Jews who challenged the inerrancy of the LXX, and claimed greater authenticity for their alternative Greek versions, led to a more self-conscious attitude and a hardening of the Christian position that 'the LXX' (by now a blanket term for all the versions in use) was the truly inspired 'word of God', to be preferred, in cases of conflict, to the Hebrew. For Christian apologists, therefore, *Ep. Arist.* and (particularly) Philo's account of LXX origins, were of great importance, for they demonstrated the inspired nature of the LXX. The miraculous elements were emphasized and elaborated, starting with Justin and Irenaeus in the second century CE and continuing to the time of Augustine in the fourth to fifth centuries, and well beyond (see Swete 1914: 13; Harl, Dorival and Munnich 1988: 47–8 for references).

The defence of the Septuagint

The earliest evidence is in Justin (d. *c.* 165), where 'the LXX' already refers to more than the Pentateuch (*Apology* 1.31). Details in *Ep. Arist.* are expanded: there is a dual embassy to Jerusalem, for instance. Justin's *Dialogue with Trypho*, in which he argues with a supposed Jewish acquaintance, asserts the superiority of the LXX over Jewish versions (68.7, 71.1–3).

Irenaeus (*c.* 130–208) is the first witness to a tradition that King Ptolemy (he thinks it was Ptolemy I) separated 'the seventy' to prevent collusion in suppressing elements of the Law (*Against Heresies* 3.21.2–3, in Eusebius *HE* 5.8.11–15). His aim is clearly apologetic; he argues for the superiority of the LXX and its divine authority over against the new Jewish versions. The fact that the seventy translators, working separately, produced identical versions, demonstrates the inspired nature of the LXX by comparison with the individual productions of the Jewish scholars, which are all different. He also emphasizes the skill of the translators. The supreme proof of the efficacy of the miraculous agreement is, however, that even the Gentiles acknowledged its divine inspiration (an indication perhaps that use was made of the legend in missionary contexts).

Clement of Alexandria (*c.* 150–211/216) follows very similar lines, as does Tertullian (*c.* 160–220). The latter, writing in Latin, is, incidentally, the first Christian author to mention *Ep. Arist.* by name. In *Apology* 18, he claims that the original Hebrew scrolls were still in the Serapeum in Alexandria, but this is rather doubtful (perhaps it was his way of vouching for the accuracy of the LXX). Another eye-witness claim, that of having seen the ruins of the translators' houses, comes in Pseudo-Justin's *Cohortatio ad Graecos* 13–15 (probably of third-century origin; see Jellicoe 1968: 44). As has been said, the tradition that the translators were put to work in separate dwellings, against the story-line of *Ep. Arist.* 301, is probably Jewish in origin, but will in any case have been developed from Philo's description of their amazing unanimity.

Early in the fourth century, Eusebius (*c.* 260–*c.* 339/340) gives a straightforward, unadorned summary of *Ep. Arist.* (*PE* 8.1–9; 9.38). Some years later, Epiphanius (367–403) provides the greatest elaboration: he includes even the apocryphal among those translated, and has the translators working not alone, but in pairs, a variation probably influenced by Luke 10.1; it is not found in any Jewish sources (*Weights and Measures* 3.6).

The Septuagint and Jewish alternatives

By now, Christians claiming that the LXX was more accurate than the Hebrew, and that divergences were the result of deliberate manipulation by the Jews (an accusation made in reverse by Jewish exegetes), had had to get to grips with the alternative Jewish versions, and with increasingly detailed textual comparisons and emendations, especially after Origen (see Chapter 5, p. 97). But however much a 'corrected' LXX was used in practice, its inspired character was maintained, so the miraculous elements in the legend were of crucial importance. The challenge of the Jewish versions was met by Irenaeus, as we have seen, with the weapon of the LXX's communal inspiration, demonstrated by the total agreement of the individual translators. In the fourth century, John Chrysostom (*c.* 347–407) claimed that the LXX had greater authority because it was translated prior to the coming of Christ, and so did not have any Christian bias, whereas the newer versions were deliberately anti-Christian by trying to discredit Christian readings (*Homily on Matthew* 5.2). A similar argument was still being mounted two centuries later by Olympiodorus (sixth century CE): the translators could not be accused of pro-Christian bias (see Pelletier 1988: 111).

Augustine and Jerome

In the light of all this, it is easy to see why Jerome's claim that the Hebrew text should form the basis for new translations because it was earlier and more authentic than the LXX, was so shocking (and even seen as a sell-out to the Jews, Brock 1972: 25), and why it drew such opposition from Augustine. These two giants of the fourth to fifth centuries crystallize the issues. For Augustine (354–430), the unanimity of the translators was essential: there was no collaboration; all were individually inspired to produce identical versions, and so the whole LXX was inspired and infallible (*City of God* 18.42–4 (not 17 as Swete 1914: 13 states); cf. *Christian Doctrine* 2.2). The passage, which is of great interest, shows how much he has to struggle to express his belief in the equal authority of both

Greek and Hebrew texts, despite the existence of discrepancies.

Already in *City of God* 15.10–13, he has discussed the question of the LXX's reliability, with examples from Genesis. He attributes discrepancies such as differences in the age of Methuselah to scribal errors which crept into the copies of the original LXX, rather than to deliberate malice on the part of the translators, who might have changed the text in order to deprive Gentiles of the truth; Augustine may perhaps be thinking of the rabbinic tradition of the Ptolemaic alterations (above, p. 74), though he does not say so. He is not altogether convinced by his own argument, since some mistakes seem to have 'a certain consistency which smacks of design rather than accident' (Bettenson 1972: 616). He ends by acknowledging that in questions of historical fact, preference should be given to the original language (15.13). The issue was important for Augustine because he saw the LXX as the vehicle of revelation to the Gentiles; hence its inspired nature was essential. Hence, too, his stress on the initiative of Ptolemy Philadelphus, the pagan king – there is no mention of Demetrius – an ironic transformation for Christian purposes of what *Ep. Arist.* originally intended for Judaism (cf. Jellicoe 1968: 44; Fernández Marcos 2000: 49).

Jerome (346–420) distances himself from the 'inspirational' approach, and looks at the LXX more dispassionately as a translation. 'Being a prophet', he says, 'and being a translator are two very different things', *aliud est enim vatem, aliud esse interpretem* (*Prologue to Genesis*). He is sceptical of the story of the translators working in separate dwellings, because this contradicts the earlier versions of *Ep. Arist.* and Josephus, who describe them as working together. He does not, that is, reject the legend out of hand, but only the deviations from the original account, which he accepts and appreciates. But the momentous step has been taken which eventually leads to the replacement, in the Western churches, of the Greek LXX by the Latin Vulgate based on translation directly from the Hebrew.

Further reading

For Philo, Colson (1966: 450–595) has Greek text and facing translation of *De Vita Mosis* References to other works by Philo are to the LCL editions. The standard Greek edition is that of Cohn and Wendland (6 vols; 1896–1930. Vol. 7, the index by Leisegang 1926, serves as a concordance, as does Borgen 2000). For general introductions and background, see especially Borgen (1992: 333–42; 1997: 14–45); Williamson (1989). Philo's use of the Bible is discussed by Amir (1988: 421–53); Borgen (1997: 46–123).

For Josephus, text and translation of *Antiquities* 12 may be found in Marcus (1933). A concordance is supplied by Rengstorf (1973–83), a bibliography by Feldman (1988a). For general introductions and background, see especially Feldman (1992: 981–98); Rajak (1983). On Josephus's use of the Bible, see Feldman (1998). Pelletier (1988) discusses Josephus's relationship to *Ep. Arist.* and to the LXX. Spottorno (1997) investigates some aspects of the text-form used by Josephus.

On the rabbinic texts, see Epstein (1935–52); Cohen (1965). For approximate dating, see Harl, Dorival and Munnich (1988: 50, 121–5). For discussions, see Fernández Marcos (2000: 45–7, 109–10, 174–86); Harl (1992: 11–20).

For sources concerning Jews in the Hellenistic and Roman periods, see Williams (1998).

On the patristic writers, Müller (1996, Chapter 4) has a useful summary and discussion. See also Fernández Marcos (2000: 48–50); Pelletier (1988: 109–11).

CHAPTER 5

Textual Developments to the Fifth Century CE

The Jewish versions

By the time Origen embarked on his great scholarly work in the mid-third century CE, there were several other Greek versions in existence alongside the LXX, of which the most influential were attributed to Aquila, Symmachus and Theodotion ('the Three'). These had emerged within Greek-speaking Judaism where they were used as alternatives to the LXX. As their readings were often cited in Jewish-Christian controversy, Christians too had to take account of them. Christian scholars were interested in these versions in non-controversial contexts also, as being supposedly new and independent translations claiming to represent the original Hebrew more faithfully. It has, however, become clear that all these 'new' versions built on earlier revisions, and there are debates as to how far they should be thought of as entirely new translations. Before looking in more detail at 'the Three', therefore, it is important to survey current research on their antecedents or 'precursors'.

The kaige *revision*

The most significant 'precursor' is what has come to be called the *kaige* revision. In 1952, a fragmentary scroll of the Minor Prophets in Greek was found in a cave at Naḥal Ḥever near the Dead Sea (8QHevXIIgr; see above, Chapter 1, p. 4). Many of the readings differed from the LXX and some scholars, especially Kahle (Chapter 3, pp. 58–9), thought at first that they represented a new translation. Barthélemy, however, realized that the text was recognizably that of the LXX, although it had been altered in many places to follow more closely a proto-Masoretic Hebrew text-type (the Hebrew source for the LXX translation of the Minor Prophets is in any case very close to the MT). The adjustments were slight, sporadic, but very distinctive.

Among the characteristics identified by Barthélemy, the most striking are: the consistent use of Greek *kai ge*, 'and indeed', to translate Hebrew (*w^e*)*gam*, '(and) also' (hence the term *kaige*); *anēr*, 'man', instead of *hekastos*, 'each one', for the idiomatic distributive sense of Hebrew *'iš*, 'man', 'each'; an ungrammatical use of *egō eimi*, 'I am', for Hebrew *'ānōkî*, 'I', followed by a finite verb, simple *egō* being kept for the Hebrew synonym *^anî*; and *ouk esti*, 'there is not', for Hebrew *'ēn*, a negative used contextually for all tenses, not just the present (for other features see Fernández Marcos 2000: 147, n. 24; 148).

Barthélemy aligned these features with similar peculiarities occurring in other places: in LXX Judges, for instance, and in some of Justin's quotations in his *Dialogue with Trypho*. He thought that the text of Lamentations, Song of Songs, Ruth and 2 Paraleipomenōn, which have *kaige* features, represented not a revision but the actual first translation. It is because it has these features in such a marked way that Ecclesiastes has sometimes been attributed to Aquila. Barthélemy's realization that the text of 8QHevXIIgr was not an isolated phenomenon, but an early example of a wider revisional trend culminating in Aquila's version, continues to influence all work on this aspect of the LXX. His 1963 monograph, *Les Devanciers d'Aquila*, has proved the impetus for what has been called 'a Copernican revolution' in Septuagint studies (cf. Bogaert 1985: 175). For he has demonstrated convincingly that, by the start of the first century CE, the LXX was sufficiently well established to form the sole basis for revisions, thus clarifying the Lagarde-Kahle dispute about Septuagint origins. 8QHevXIIgr also proves that there was a concern, in some circles at least, to adjust the older

Greek to a particular form of Hebrew, and that exact reproduction of the Hebrew was a growing concern. At the same time, it demonstrates how seriously the LXX was taken by at least some Palestinian Jews (Bogaert 1985: 181).

The scroll was initially dated to the mid-first century CE; this, together with its distinctive *kaige* traits, led Barthélemy to situate it within the context of first-century Palestinian rabbinic exegesis, which flourished under Hillel and culminated in Aquila in the second century (1963: 271). But the date has now been more plausibly assigned to the second half of the first century BCE (Parsons 1990: 26). This means that the historical setting and *Sitz im Leben* are less clear-cut than Barthélemy supposed. In fact, the main criticism of Barthélemy's innovative work is that it ties up too many loose threads in one go (we will see this again with Theodotion; below p. 84).

Munnich (1987) has moved the debate forward by situating the *kaige* text-type itself in a wider context. He suggests that literary and stylistic concerns also played a part, though in a non-systematic way. He thinks this trend begins with LXX Psalms, a translation which then influenced subsequent texts. There are also theological and exegetical interests at work, but these are not necessarily to be linked with specifically Palestinian interests, where these can be identified. Munnich's important contribution is discussed in Fernández Marcos (2000: 152); Gentry (1995: 417–18, with bibliography, n. 119; 1998: 221–2, 226–7, with qualifications). Gentry broadens the horizons still further by situating these early textual developments in the context of 'the constant interchange between Diasporan and Palestinian Judaism' (1998: 227).

A word needs to be said about terminology. I have spoken about a *kaige* 'revision'; Barthélemy's designation is 'group'. But the term '*kaige* recension' is also frequently found. A recension is a text which gives evidence of thorough-going and systematic editing. In the present case, however, it is misleading; the evidence does not suggest an organized project. '*Kaige*' is, rather, a kind of shorthand for a particular trend with wide, but loose, ramifications. Gentry too rejects the term 'recension': 'Instead, one must envisage a continuum from the Greek Pentateuch all the way to Aquila in which approaches and attitudes to translation are trying to find ways of bringing the Greek into a closer quantitative alignment with the Hebrew' (1998: 228–9; cf. 1995: 497; Wevers 1988: 33–4).

One of the revolutionary aspects of Barthélemy's work is his thesis that Theodotion, traditionally a late-second-century translator and the last-named of 'the Three', actually belonged to his (supposed) first-century CE *kaige* revisers; in fact, he identified him with Jonathan ben 'Uzziel, who wrote a Targum to the Prophets, and made him the head of the 'school' (hence the term '*kaige*-Theodotion' is sometimes used). This is very controversial, but, even if we remain open to the existence of a real second-century Theodotion, it has become clear that he was building on much earlier material. For this reason 'Theodotion' – among the most complicated areas of LXX study today – will be discussed before the other members of 'the Three'.

'Theodotion'

It is now clear that 'Theodotion' (θ') covers a number of different entities. The Christian sources are inconsistent. The earliest, Irenaeus, says that Theodotion was a Jewish proselyte from Ephesus, who translated the Hebrew Scriptures into Greek (*Against Heresies* 3.21.1). Epiphanius seems to have confused him with Aquila by having him come from Pontus; he also says he was a disciple there of Marcion (*Weights and Measures* 17). This would date him to about 140 CE. Jerome calls him an Ebionite (*Famous Men* 54; the Ebionites were a Jewish-Christian sect regarded as heretical). Both Epiphanius and Jerome stress that Theodotion, though translating the Hebrew, also kept close to the LXX: this is the nearest we come to the true picture of a revision against the Hebrew.

The main characteristic of the readings traditionally ascribed to Theodotion is a tendency to transliterate obscure Hebrew words (names of animals, trees, etc.) and technical terms, especially where the cult is involved, although the practice is not wholly consistent. Apart from this, there are no particularly striking features: the translation is close to the

Hebrew but without doing violence to the Greek. If a *kaige*
setting is posited, then the characteristics of this group, as
sketched above, must be looked for too. The general *kaige*
trend is present in Job (Gentry 1995: 496), in Exodus and in
Joshua (O'Connell, Greenspoon; both in Fernández Marcos
2000: 147, n. 23); but it is minimal for the Minor Prophets
(Gentry 1998: 220–1), and there is disagreement as to whether
Daniel Th. (see above, Chapter 1, p. 23) exhibits *kaige* traits.
What seems certain is that many of these readings date from
the first century BCE/CE, not the second CE.

   With the exception of Daniel Th. (if this really belongs to
the corpus, see below, p. 86), the version has only survived in
fragments and isolated readings, preserved as marginal glosses
in later manuscripts of the LXX, or in quotations by patristic
writers. The most substantial remains are in manuscripts of
Proverbs, Isaiah, Jeremiah, Ezekiel and, especially, Job. Here,
the readings identified as Theodotionic cover the portions of
text absent from the LXX; this shows that Theodotion's
version was aligned to the MT, not just a revision of the
traditional LXX. Theodotionic readings occur in the NT (e.g.
Dan. 6.23 in Heb. 11.33; Dan. 7.13 in Mark 14.62; often in
Rev.; cf. Ulrich 2000: 334–5) and in early-second-century
sources (including Justin, Clement of Rome, *Shepherd of Hermas*
and *Letter of Barnabas*). As there are doubts about the
relationship of Daniel Th. to the rest of Theodotion, it would
be better to concentrate on examples from other books to
establish identity; this, however, is very difficult, as the
character of Theodotion has been largely determined by
Daniel.

   The picture, although clearer, is not yet complete. Several
different positions are still discernible. Some scholars follow
Barthélemy in concluding that there was no second-century
'Theodotion', only a first-century *kaige*-like reviser (whom he
called 'R'). The terms 'proto-' or 'Ur-'Theodotion should be
dropped, and the patristic evidence ignored (e.g. Gentry,
McLay); others, however, still use this terminology (e.g
Munnich, Greenspoon). Others again accept that Theodotionic readings originate with the pre-Christian *kaige* movement,
but posit a second stage in the second century, to make sense

of the patristic identifications (e.g. Jobes and Silva 2000: 41–2, a good summary, though the scholarly consensus is perhaps exaggerated; Fernández Marcos 2000: 148–50, who also thinks that traditions about a second-century Theodotion are too firmly established to be entirely ignored).

There are at least two further complications. First, there is the conundrum of Daniel Th. The LXX differs so markedly from the MT that even the Christian churches adopted Daniel Th., which was known to be much closer to the Hebrew. This seems to have happened in the second half of the third century, perhaps under the influence of Origen, as both versions were in circulation up till then and LXX Daniel survives in the pre-Origenic Papyrus 967. Daniel Th., as well as Daniel LXX, was known to NT writers, so it was not a late-second-century innovation. There is also some uncertainty as to how Daniel Th. relates to the other early Theodotionic evidence; it may be that we have another originally independent reviser who later became identified as 'Theodotion'; and to confuse the issue still further, some have argued that 'Theodotion' here is really Symmachus (see Fernández Marcos 2000: 137). There is also disagreement as to whether Daniel Th. represents a revision (until now the majority view) or a new translation. McLay finds little dependence on the LXX and thinks we have an independent translation (1998: 253–4). All of this indicates the complexity and interrelatedness of scribal activity in these early centuries, of which we have only sketchy knowledge (Fernández Marcos 2000: 138).

Secondly, some of the readings attributed by Origen to Theodotion clearly come from a different source, since they are full of conflations and expansions. The readings for the Minor Prophets are a case in point; this was first noted by Barthélemy, though not all agree. For Judges, however, Bodine (1980) identified the Theodotionic readings as consonant with a second-century Hebraizing text (i.e. the Theodotion of the putative sources), quite different from the first-century *kaige* text which he identified in the 'LXX' of Vaticanus. This confirms Barthélemy; the outcome is that the LXX of Judges itself is best preserved in the Antiochian text and the OL (see Chapter 1, p. 16; Bodine 1980). The Theodotionic readings for some sections of Samuel-Kings are really the work of Theodoret of Cyrrhus, who, like Theodotion, is identified in some manuscripts by the Greek letter theta (θ); these readings were then erroneously attributed to Theodotion by copyists (Fernández Marcos 2000: 145). Sorting out the different strands of the Theodotionic readings, especially if Daniel Th. is excluded, and clarifying their relationship to the *kaige* texts, is a difficult but essential enterprise. For the moment, we must be aware that readings attributed to Theodotion do not necessarily come from the same source. What is clear, and significant, is that there are very early roots to this supposedly second-century CE version, which then attracted and absorbed further similar material. As will be seen with Aquila and Symmachus, the dividing line between making a new translation and revising or developing existing prototypes, becomes increasingly blurred.

Aquila

Traditionally, the earliest of the supposed new versions was attributed to Aquila (α'), though it now has to yield its place to 'Theodotion'. Both Christian and Jewish sources agree that Aquila had been a pagan from Sinope on the Black Sea (though Epiphanius makes him an Ephesian, probably wrongly; *Weights and Measures* 14). Christian tradition describes him as having been converted to Christianity in Jerusalem, but excommunicated because he would not give up astrology. He then became a Jew, learnt Hebrew, and set about retranslating the Scriptures in order to discredit the LXX. A less 'tabloid' kind of assessment is found in Origen and Jerome, writers interested in textual criticism, who admired his skills as a translator. His work, according to Epiphanius, was done about 128–29 CE. This is accepted by Barthélemy (1963: 144), though other scholars think the task was so enormous that it was probably finished rather later, perhaps about 140 CE. In Palestinian Jewish sources (*y. Meg.* 1.11; *y. Kidd.* 1.1), he is simply called a proselyte, not a discredited Christian. He is said to have been a pupil of famous early rabbis, especially Akiba (fl. 95–135). Some scholars (especially Barthélemy 1963: 3–21) think that his translation reflects the exegetical practices of Akiba, though others are less convinced. The Babylonian Talmud and the Tosefta speak of a person called Onqelos, the supposed author of a Targum of the Pentateuch, who is often identified with Aquila, though others think the Onqelos stories have been modelled on those of Aquila; where the identification is accepted, some think that the authorship of the Targum is a secondary development.

Aquila's version, of which only fragments and isolated readings remain, is marked by its quantitative closeness to the Hebrew. In places, he reproduces Hebrew idioms to the detriment of Greek grammar and syntax, and he often attempts to use the same Greek equivalent consistently for a given Hebrew word; this sometimes results in renderings inappropriate to the context. The extreme literalness is often taken to show Aquila's reverence for the Hebrew text, and this may have been a factor. It has also been argued that the version was intended to help mainly Greek-speaking Jews to gain access to the Hebrew text (cf. above, Chapter 3, p. 53). This would certainly make sense during the final tragic stages of Jewish rebellion against Rome, when Hebrew, as the traditional holy language, was being more actively promoted. Indeed, much of Aquila's version might have been nearly incomprehensible apart from its Hebrew counterpart. It is more likely to have been a response to inner-Jewish developments than a tool designed specifically for use in controversy with Christians, although it did prove useful in this respect.

Two general provisos need to be made. First, Aquila is by no means as inflexibly literal as he is usually said to be (see Barthélemy 1963: 15–21; Barr 1979: 312; Grabbe 1982: 529). Secondly, he has not invented his distinctive style but developed the *kaige* approach already discernible from the first century BCE onwards, as we have seen. Aquila's most significant extant 'precursor' is 8QHevXIIgr. Thanks to Barthélemy, Aquila has been recognized as an extreme development of the *kaige* style of revision. This means that features in LXX Ecclesiastes, previously thought to indicate his hand, probably reflect an earlier translator in the same line.

The question of Aquila's relationship to the *kaige* movement now needs to be examined in the context of the Jewish versions as a whole and of their place in the development of rabbinic exegesis. Nonetheless, it was Aquila's version which was most popular in Jewish use as an alternative to the traditional LXX, even for synagogal readings, for as long as Greek remained the chief language of the western Empire, that is, until the Arab invasions of the seventh century. Christian scholars, too, used Aquila in their own writings as a supposedly reliable witness to what the Hebrew 'really' said, even if this concern remained peripheral to their theological and exegetical agenda.

Symmachus

Faithful to 'the' Hebrew, but more natural and even elegant in its Greek style, Symmachus's version (σ') was greatly appreciated by Christian writers, though there is less evidence for its popularity in Jewish sources, which seldom mention it. The dating is uncertain, as the Christian sources, especially Eusebius and Epiphanius, give conflicting accounts; late-second or early-third century CE is most likely; the version is probably the latest of the three. The absence of any mention in Irenaeus is usually taken to indicate that the version must be later than 190 CE, but Swete (1914: 49) rightly counsels caution over this argument from silence. Symmachus is variously described as an Ebionite, or as a disaffected Samaritan who became a Jew; again, some of the details seem calculated to cast slurs on his character. Earlier scholarship opted for the Ebionite identification, but the prevailing view now, from a careful evaluation of the sources, and especially from the evidence of the version itself, is that the Jewish character of Symmachus's work is beyond doubt. He may just possibly be the Sumkos ben Joseph, disciple of R. Meir, mentioned in rabbinic texts (Salvesen 1991: 294); in any case, he reflects current Palestinian rabbinic exegesis in many places. That a version which combined a reliable translation of the proto-Masoretic text with acceptable Greek was made at the end of the second century indicates that there was still a place for the

Greek Bible in western Judaism; if the motive had just been to show Christians how erroneous the LXX was, Aquila's version would surely have been sufficient.

As with Theodotion, Symmachus seems to have had antecedents. Readings attributed to him have been identified in a number of earlier texts, including the NT, Sirach and Josephus's text for Samuel-Kings; there also seem to be links with the *kaige* group (Fernández Marcos 2000: 133–9). Despite this, the surviving material (the most substantial portions are in Psalms and the Pentateuch) is so distinctive that, more than with the other two versions, it can be described as a new translation rather than a revision; in fact, there is disagreement as to how far Symmachus used the traditional LXX at all.

Other Jewish versions

As well as 'the Three', fragments of other, less well-known versions have survived, either in readings from Origen's Hexapla or from references in patristic works. These include:

1. *The 'Quinta'*, or 'Fifth Translation' (i.e. additional to the LXX and 'the Three'). Readings have been identified for Kingdoms, Job, Psalms (where they are best attested), Song of Songs and the Minor Prophets, though not the Pentateuch. Not all the attributions are secure. Some links with the *kaige* group have been found for Psalms (see Venetz in Fernández Marcos 2000: 157), and for the Minor Prophets where Barthélemy identified the Quinta as the *kaige* revision. Howard (1974) pointed out some difficulties with this identification and concluded that the Quinta here is akin to, but not identical with, the *kaige* group; Barthélemy, however, maintained his position (see Bogaert 1993: 633). The debate well illustrates the difficult and delicate nature of defining textual affiliations (cf. Gentry 1995: 497).

2. *'The Hebrew'*. This designation is sometimes a way of referring to the Hebrew text, especially in Jerome, but in some places, according to Fernández Marcos, it refers to a specific version, at least in Genesis, Job, Ezekiel and

perhaps Exodus and Deuteronomy. It seems to be closer in style to Symmachus than to Aquila (2000: 162–3).

3. *'The Syrian'* is a mysterious source, mentioned in some of the patristic commentators, though not Origen. There is debate as to whether it represents a translation, by a Syrian scholar, from the Peshitta (the less likely view) or from the Hebrew (so Field, Rahlfs, Ziegler). Sprenger thought that a Syrian had translated the Hebrew into Syriac (not Greek) but that this translation had later been displaced by the Peshitta. Guinot thought the readings quoted by Theodoret came from the Peshitta or something closely akin. All these suggestions are very tentative; there is still no consensus (see Fernández Marcos 2000: 164–7).

4. *'The Samaritan'.* There is much uncertainty as to the provenance of readings attributed by Origen to 'the Samaritan (version)', but the fragmentary Papyrus Giessen and a Samaritan synagogue inscription from Thessalonica have convinced some scholars that there was a complete translation of the Samaritan Pentateuch which Origen could have used. The appearance of Garizim for Ebal in Deut. 27.4 probably clinches the Samaritan character. Others think that these readings come from revisions of the LXX made by and for the Samaritan community. Either way, these obscure fragments point to a distinctive Samaritan textual tradition in Greek which found its way into Christian scholarship and is a reminder of the complexity of religious activity and interaction in the third century (see Fernández Marcos 2000: 167–9; cf. Ulrich 2000: 325–6, on Jewish 'proto-Samaritan' texts in Hebrew at Qumran).

5. *The 'Sexta' and 'Septima'*, the 'Sixth' and 'Seventh' (versions) are also mentioned by Origen and others, but they are very poorly preserved.

In summary, these, and still other remnants, are tantalizing evidence for the multiplicity of forms in which the Greek Scriptures circulated during the early Christian centuries:

'they comprise valuable documents which reflect moments of intense philological activity around the Greek Bible' (Fernández Marcos 2000: 155). Much of the evidence has been gathered in Field (1875) and in the second apparatus of the Göttingen editions. New material now needs to be added, and the old in some cases reassessed; an important project is under way to produce an updated 'Field', which will include electronic resources (Norton 1997; Jobes and Silva 2000: 317).

Christian use of the versions

Given the emergence of important versions within Judaism, it is ironic that what has survived of them is in Christian writings. This may first have been because controversies over the correct rendering of key passages and the relative authority of the Hebrew and Greek Scriptures forced Christian apologists to take on board alternative readings. As we have seen (above, Chapter 4, pp. 76–7), some Christian writers tried to defend the superior status of the LXX, the work of 'the Seventy', against versions produced only by individuals. In this context, it is perhaps significant that many sources mention unorthodox backgrounds for 'the Three': they were Samaritans, Ebionites, apostates, astrologers, and so on. The suspicion arises that the aim was to cast doubt on their credibility. On the other hand, their Christian connections, however questionable or short-lived, could have served to make them more acceptable to Christian readers. It was necessary to make use of this sensitive material; but Christian apologists needed to have some sense of control over it. The accounts of Eusebius, Epiphanius and others are not neutral, and this is a reason for not relying too much on their biographical information. The embarrassment which Christian writers sometimes show in their treatment of the versions is well illustrated by Jerome's use of Symmachus: he admires his translation and uses it often (e.g. in his *Commentary on Amos*, see Dines 1992: 108; 1998: 432–3). But he sometimes refers to the versions as of unorthodox origin and therefore unreliable (cf. Kamesar 1993: 68–9, who brings out this double standard especially with regard to Aquila).

But the versions were not only used in controversy. They also gave Christians ignorant of Hebrew some access, however inaccurate, to the Hebrew text, even if they continued to assert the superiority of the LXX. Doctrinaire positions apart, Christian writers often used readings from the versions in their efforts to interpret the LXX even in pastoral, homiletic and exegetical works designed for other Christians.

The Christian recensions

Although there were no Christian attempts to produce new translations until Jerome's Hebrew-Latin innovations in the fourth to fifth centuries, the habit of revising and 'correcting' the existing LXX continued in Christian contexts. Some of these revisions, or 'recensions', constitute systematic editions associated with specific times, places and people (for a helpful introduction, see Wevers 1988: 30–3). As with the Jewish versions, these Christian recensions have, in some cases, turned out to be carriers of much older material.

By the mid-third century, the use of the LXX in doctrinal debates between Christians, as well as in encounters (not always hostile) with Jewish scholars, had become complicated by the fact that there were so many different forms of the text in circulation. What any given part of the Christian world called 'the LXX' was in fact a disparate collection of manuscripts marked by earlier revisions as well as by the inevitable textual corruptions that resulted from manual copying. This can be seen in the major uncial manuscripts of the fourth and fifth centuries, none of which preserves a pure or consistent text (Vaticanus is on the whole the soundest witness, but this cannot be taken for granted; see above, Chapter 1, pp. 6–7).

Until recently, it was customary to organize manuscript evidence according to three supposed Christian recensions described in the late-fourth century by Jerome. In the Prologue to his *Commentary on Paraleipomenōn* he says that, in his day, there was much confusion among Christians because different regions used different 'editions' of the Bible. The western churches, around Palestine, used Pamphilus's version;

the eastern ones, around Syria, Lucian's; and the southern ones, around Egypt, that of Hesychius. Each of the individuals named is presented as a third-century martyr; evidently martyrdom, now a thing of the past, provided impeccable credentials for associated texts; at first glance, this is quite different from the way the Jewish versions were presented. But Jerome's apparently edifying picture contains a thinly veiled polemic: he does not regard this plurality as a good thing, and it may be that his references at least to Hesychius and Lucian are slightly mocking (cf. Kamesar 1993: 56). At any rate, Jerome promotes the Palestinian text as the most scientific and accurate (cf. Dines 1998: 422, n. 6). Fernández Marcos suggests that the Lucianic Recension was made in conscious competition with the Palestinian text and refers to a passage from Pseudo-Chrysostom on Isa. 9.6, quoted by Ziegler (1939: 73); Pseudo-Chrysostom claimed that Lucian had not added or subtracted anything and that his text was a more faithful witness to the Hebrew than the Palestinian one (Fernández Marcos 2000: 196, with n. 22). This defence of Lucian is probably a reaction to criticisms, found elsewhere in Jerome, that the other recensions played fast and loose with the sacred text (see Fernández Marcos 2000: 224, nn. 7, 8 for references). That there were doctrinal and exegetical rivalries between different Christian churches is well known; it is interesting to glimpse that these extended to the choice of text-forms, each of which was claimed as the authentic LXX (see Jerome, *Letter to Sunius and Fretela* 2). But there are other reasons for treating Jerome's account of the threefold tradition with caution, particularly where 'Hesychius' is concerned.

The 'Hesychian Recension'

Swete accepts Jerome's claim as basically trustworthy (1914: 78–9) and Jellicoe thinks there is sufficient evidence for such a revision (1968: 345–6). But the identity of this Hesychius remains obscure and there is insufficient manuscript evidence for a distinctively Egyptian type of revision, so most scholars are now sceptical that there was ever a 'Hesychian Recension', in the sense of a systematic reworking of the LXX undertaken by the Egyptian Church. They prefer to speak of an 'Alexandrian' or 'Egyptian' group of manuscripts. Some have pointed to Vaticanus, Sinaiticus and Alexandrinus (Skeat 1999, however, argues for a Palestinian provenance for B and S). What Jerome seems to refer to are sporadic local textual characteristics, with which he has associated an otherwise unknown local martyr, although there was an Egyptian bishop called Hesychius who was martyred in the great persecution under Diocletian, *c.* 303 CE. If this was the person Jerome had in mind, he may have known more about his work as a biblical scholar than has come down to us, or he may have picked on him as a suitable figurehead, to match Pamphilus (*c.* 240–309; also martyred under Diocletian) and Lucian (a churchman – though not altogether 'orthodox' – martyred in *c.* 312 under Maximin Daza). Distinctive 'Egyptian' readings have also been claimed for the early-third-century Papyrus 965, the Bohairic version, and some patristic writings, especially Cyril of Alexandria's *Commentary on the Minor Prophets* (*c.* 425) and Didymus the Blind's *Commentary on Zachariah* (*c.* 387). Distinctive features seem to be: a preference for short readings, the presevation of the old word order, some free renderings not conditioned by the Hebrew, and a number of idiosyncratic readings. These features, however, do not add up to criteria for identifying a recension. For the moment, the manuscript evidence does not provide a coherent picture, although in places very early readings may have been preserved. In particular, it seems that Vaticanus should not be associated with this text-type, at least for the Octateuch, Tobit and Daniel Th. The picture may become clearer as more work is done on the growing body of Egyptian papyri, which could provide better evidence for the nature of the Greek reflected in our sources, and as the historical books of the LXX are gradually published by Göttingen (see Fernández Marcos 2000: 241–6).

The Hexaplaric Recension

The 'edition' attributed by Jerome to Pamphilus is the only one of the three which is an unambiguous work of planned

revision. The attribution to Pamphilus is misleading, as the
initiative, and probably the work itself, came from Pamphilus's
friend and teacher, Origen. As, however, the revised texts were
disseminated by Pamphilus and by Eusebius, bishop of
Caesarea, it is not quite certain that they did not make further
adjustments (Jenkins 1998a: 85). But by the time Jerome was
writing, at the end of the fourth century, Origen's orthodoxy
was suspect and, although Jerome had the greatest admiration
for Origen as a scholar, he was circumspect in his references.
Pamphilus had untainted credentials, including martyrdom,
and this is probably the reason for the attribution (Origen is
not counted as a martyr, even though his death in *c.* 253
followed resistance and torture during the persecution of
Decius).

Origen (*c.* 185–253/4), a brilliant biblical scholar, theolo-
gian and philosopher, had been teacher, then director, at the
renowned catechetical and exegetical school in Alexandria,
but moved to Caesarea, the Roman capital of Palestine, in
c. 234, where he founded a similar school and library. This was
a period of relative peace and stability for the Church (only
disturbed by a wave of persecution under Maximin the
Thracian, 235–38) until the advent of Decius in 249. Caesarea
contained a small Christian church and more sizeable Jewish
and Samaritan communities, but it was first and foremost a
pagan city. The Christian church was growing, but was still a
minority presence and felt itself vulnerable to opposition from
both pagans and Jews. On an intellectual level, there was much
debate and controversy between Jewish and Christian scholars
and teachers, not always acrimonious. Origen, although
conventional in attacking Jewish beliefs and exegesis in his
writings, had many Jewish friends, and was in close touch with
various rabbis from whom he learned much current *halakah*
and *haggadah* (some of which, otherwise unrecorded, he has
unwittingly preserved). He learned some Hebrew, though was
probably never very proficient; in any case, most dialogue
would have taken place in Greek, since this was still the normal
spoken and written language for Jews and Christians alike, and
most biblical exegesis would have involved the use of Greek
texts (cf. Harl 1992: 19–20).

The Hexapla

In this context, Origen realized that Christian exegetes were at
a disadvantage in basing their arguments on a text (probably a
version of the LXX very close to that now found, for most
books, in Vaticanus) which differed in many places from the
Hebrew texts and the Greek translations, especially Aquila's,
used by the rabbis. To put Christian exegetes and apologists in
a stronger position, he undertook a gigantic enterprise (see his
Letter to Africanus, c. 240). He set about correlating all available
textual material in a six-column synopsis which for that reason
came to be called the Hexapla ('six-fold'). This was designed
to function as a resource for Christian scholars and teachers
who needed, for instance, to know how to handle the
doctrinally important proof-text Isa. 7.14, among many others.
It was not intended to replace the traditional LXX as the text
used by Christians (Origen himself went on using it in his
pastoral works). This apologetic aim apart, it is very likely that
Origen's scholarly instincts encouraged him to provide the
best textual evidence he could for the use of other scholars.

The Hexapla is no longer extant, and there are some
doubts as to its actual arrangement and content, but our
sources, especially Jerome, give the following picture. For each
translated book of the LXX the columns were arranged as
follows:

Column 1:	a word or short phrase in unpointed Hebrew.
Column 2:	the same word(s), transliterated into Greek, with vowels added.
Column 3:	Aquila's rendering of the word/phrase (perhaps placed here because of its closeness to the Hebrew).
Column 4:	Symmachus's version (also understood to be a reliable rendering of the Hebrew).
Column 5:	the reading of the LXX according to the textform used by Origen.
Column 6:	the reading of 'Theodotion' (perhaps as reflecting the Hebrew while supposedly remaining close to the LXX). This was used as the main source of 'corrections'.

Readings from any other available versions (Quinta, Samaritan, etc.) were added in two additional columns as needed, or (more probably) incorporated into the sixth column (cf. Jenkins 1998b: 91).

From what was effectively a pre-electronic database, it would have been possible to see at a glance how the LXX related to other versions, and thus to the original Hebrew (it did not occur to anyone at this time that the Hebrew underlying the LXX was sometimes different). There is no firm date for the production of the Hexapla, but the decade between 235 and 245 is the most likely time. The finished product, in a series of codices hand-written in Origen's scriptorium by professional scribes, must have been immense. It was probably never copied in its entirety, though surviving fragments show that at least some parts (most likely individual books) were in circulation. Jerome claims to have read it from cover to cover, twice, in the library at Caesarea in order to obtain a corrected text of the OT (*Commentary on Titus* 3.9; *Commentary on Psalms* 1; Kelly 1975: 135); he may have exaggerated his own thoroughness, but there is no reason to doubt that he saw and made use of it in exactly the way Origen had intended: for checking on the accuracy of the Greek manuscripts.

The original copy seems to have remained in the library at Caesarea until the city came under Arab rule in 638, but nothing is known about its fate. Very little has survived in tabular form, and nothing with all six columns. The most substantial find so far is the Ambrosian Palimpsest (1098), which contains Columns 2 to 6 for about one hundred and fifty verses of Psalms 17(18) to 88(89). It was found in Milan in 1896 by Mercati, and published in 1958; for an example covering Psalm 27(28).6–8, see Würthwein 1980: 188. There is no trace of Column 1 (the Hebrew lemma), and Column 6 contains not Theodotion but the Quinta. Another palimpsest (2005), found by C. Taylor in the Cairo Genizah, and published in 1900, preserves fragments of Psalm 21(22).15–18. This time both Columns 1 and 6 are missing, but Jenkins has demonstrated convincingly that they were accidentally lost when the parchment was cut for reuse (1998b: 91). Other hexaplaric snippets are found in manuscripts as marginal notes; an example taken from 86 (ninth century), which lacks only the Hebrew of Column 1, can be seen in Ziegler's edition of the Minor Prophets, in the second apparatus for Hos. 11.1 (1943: 172). A manuscript with fragments of Aquila's version of 3 Kgdms 20.7–17; 4 Kgdms 23.12–27, was published by Burkitt in 1897, but for the most part the manuscript glosses give only isolated readings from the other versions. The most ample source of hexaplaric evidence is the Syro-Hexaplar, a literal Syriac translation of the fifth column with marginal notes giving the versional readings, made by Paul of Tella in 616 CE.

There are a number of unresolved questions concerning the original Hexapla and its purpose.

(1) The Tetrapla. In various sources a 'Tetrapla' is mentioned. This has been variously identified as (1) an earlier work, either by Origen, or used by him as a prototype, comprising only the LXX and 'the Three', possibly of Jewish origin; or (2) a shortened version of the Hexapla without the first two columns; or (3) a way of referring to the Hexapla, but betraying how it was actually used (i.e. only Columns 3 to 6 were of interest). There is no consensus on this issue.

(2) The first column. The existence of the first column is sometimes questioned. As none of the extant fragments show a column with Hebrew characters, some (especially Nautin) have doubted whether it ever existed even in the original Hexapla. Probably, however, Christian scribes were unable to copy Hebrew and so omitted the lemma; in any case, they reproduced the Greek transliterations which rendered the Hebrew unnecessary. Origen himself was either competent to write Hebrew or could call on Jewish expertise; his initial work of scholarly comparison required the presence of the Hebrew to demonstrate that the text used was that in current Jewish use (Norton 1998: 112). And too little of the Hexapla has survived for us to assume that the omission of the first column was typical of all copied extracts.

(3) The second column. There is uncertainty about the nature and purpose of the second column. Were Greek transliterations already in circulation as an aid to Jews who did not know much Hebrew? Or were they made on purpose to match the Hebrew in Column 1 (supposing that to have existed)? Were they to alert Greek readers to Hebrew words not represented in the LXX (but Aquila's version would have done this)? Were they intended to provide a vocalized form of the unpointed Hebrew, reproducing, as far as Greek was able, the current conventions of Hebrew pronunciation? Or were they to enable non-Hebrew-speakers to pronounce the Hebrew lemma? The last two suggestions are closely connected and seem plausible: an ability to say the Hebrew words aloud during debates with Jewish scholars could have been important for Christian apologists. If the Greek was to enable pronunciation, it would presumably have echoed the Hebrew written and spoken in contemporary Caesarea. Retroversions, where they can be made, result in something very close to the MT; they are sometimes supplied as the missing first column, though this is a methodologically questionable practice.

(4) The fifth column. The most serious question, however, concerns exactly what appeared in the fifth column (the LXX). Origen's intention was to provide an edition which showed, through the adaptation of standard text-critical marks (called Aristarchian, after Aristarchus, the third-century BCE Alexandrian scholar who invented them), how the LXX differed from the Hebrew. Words or longer passages in the LXX which were lacking in the Hebrew were marked with a sign called an obelus (used by Aristarchus to indicate doubtful readings in Homer and other classical texts). Material in the Hebrew which was lacking in the LXX was added from the other versions, usually 'Theodotion', and marked by an asterisk (used by Aristarchus to indicate readings of special interest). Both types of divergence were marked at the end by another sign called a metobelus. Some manuscripts have preserved these 'hexaplaric signs'; see Würthwein (1980: 190) for an example from the fifth-century Codex Colberto-

Sarravianus; another extract is printed by Swete (1914: 73). 'Normalizations' against the MT would also have meant the inclusion of passages not found in the traditional LXX; some of them, for instance in Job and Jeremiah, were substantial (on the so-called 'asterisked' additions to Job, see Gentry 1995). Significantly, however, Origen did not omit the LXX's 'pluses', saying that he did not 'dare' to do this to the traditional hallowed text (*Commentary on Matthew* 15.14).

Certainly such an edition was made. It circulated widely, and became extremely popular. When Constantine established his new capital at Constantinople in 330 CE, he is said to have commissioned fifty copies of the Bible from the scriptorium at Caesarea for the churches there. Even allowing for exaggeration, it was undoubtedly a moment of increased copying of the Bible. It is this critically corrected LXX that Jerome means by his 'Pamphilian edition'.

What is unclear, and disputed, is whether the critical marks and adjustments already occurred in the Hexapla itself. Did the fifth column show the LXX 'corrected', and carrying the text-critical signs, or not? There are serious arguments on both sides. The absence of critical signs in the Ambrosian Palimpsest or the Genizah fragments has been taken to indicate that there were none in the original fifth column (e.g. Mercati and Fernández Marcos); but Nautin's view is that this argument from silence does not hold against various key passages in Origen, Eusebius and Jerome (see Schaper 1998: 6–9). A more compelling argument is that a 'corrected' fifth column would have been both unwieldy and unnecessary: the pluses, minuses and other variations could be seen synoptically in the parallel versions. The balance of probability is that there were no critical signs in the Hexapla, and that Origen, or Pamphilus and Eusebius, made the critical edition separately (see Fernández Marcos 2000: 213–15); Schaper, however, prefers to leave the question open (1998: 9). In any case, the synoptic presentation of the Hexapla was of limited scope: it could only show straightforward divergences. But Origen also had to cope with places where word order was different, whole passages were transposed (as in Jeremiah) or omitted (Job), or with paraphrastic translations (Isaiah, Proverbs). It makes more sense to suppose that he tackled all of this separately. But we really have very little idea of how the Hexapla presented books like Jeremiah, Job or Isaiah.

Whatever the Hexapla's original format, the new edition, brought into line with the Hebrew, soon dominated the field, although the existence of rival versions, especially the Lucianic, shows that this did not happen all at once (cf. Kamesar 1993: 35). Origen had not intended his work to be used indiscriminately; it was to help users of the Bible who needed a clearer picture of the text in order to gain access to the Hebrew, whether for debate or for pastoral and homiletic purposes. However methodologically unacceptable by modern standards, his was a work of meticulous scholarship, under-taken, one guesses, largely from love of the textual enterprise itself.

But it was not long before things got out of hand: copies of the hexaplaric edition were made in which the critical marks were inaccurately copied, or not copied at all, probably because scribes did not understand their significance. The end result was that the clear distinctions between orignal LXX and versions in the Hexapla itself, not to mention Origen's own rearrangements, became blurred so that what now passed for 'the LXX' was in fact a badly corrupted text. As the hexaplaric version was believed to be the genuine one (because of its supposed closeness to 'the' Hebrew), and was very widely disseminated, the consequences for textual study of the LXX were catastrophic. Very many manuscripts were affected, from the end of the third century onwards, some more drastically than others, and this has contributed to our difficulties in reconstructing the original text. Pre-Origenic material is thus of enormous interest, although this may itself betray other forms of revision, and often does: the third-century Washington Papyrus of the Minor Prophets, for instance, is marked by the *kaige* trend. Important, too, is the witness of other text-forms – particularly the Antiochian/ Lucianic – perhaps promoted in conscious rivalry to Origen's. At any rate, the Hexaplaric Recension did not completely obliterate other traditions. And there is much for which to be grateful: Origen was in fact instrumental in preserving much precious Jewish textual and exegetical material that would otherwise have been lost.

The Lucianic (Antiochian) Recension

Jerome's reference is probably to Lucian of Antioch (*c.* 250 – *c.* 312). He was Syrian, but knew Greek and perhaps a little Hebrew. He did some of his studies in Caesarea, where Origen's work was being continued by Eusebius and Pamphilus, and where the Hexapla was now kept in the library. He was the founder of an equally prestigious exegetical 'school' at Antioch, though his career as a churchman was chequered and for some time he may even have been excommunicated (the circumstances are obscure; Theodoret may not have been speaking literally when he described him as *aposunagōgos*, 'removed from the synagogue', *HE* 1.3; cf. John 9.22; 16.2; Fernández Marcos 2000: 223, n. 2). By the time of his martyrdom, however, he had been reinstated, though no contemporary sources state that he edited a revision of the LXX.

The recension bearing his name is associated nowadays with the churches dependent on fourth-century Antioch. It constitutes one of the most complicated issues in LXX studies. Something very distinctive can be identified in certain manuscripts as well as in biblical citations in John Chrysostom, Theodoret of Cyrrhus (both also from fourth-century Antioch) and others. But the identification, in some pre-Christian papyri and in Josephus, of similar types of readings (sometimes anachronistically called 'proto-Lucianic') has both underlined the importance of this text-type and cast doubt on whether the third-century CE Lucian ever undertook a systematic revision of the LXX. If he did, he was basing it on earlier models, but to what extent is not yet clear. Many scholars today prefer to speak of an 'Antiochian (or 'Antiochene') Text' rather than a 'Lucianic Recension', because this allows for wider manuscript affiliations (the manuscripts involved are, however, still designated by an 'L' in critical apparatuses).

One of the chief characteristics of this text-type is the replacing of Koine forms with those of the more literary Attic Greek. Although a marked feature of third-century CE literary taste, it was already a factor in the first century BCE, so cannot be used as an absolute criterion for distinguishing between early and late strata. A move to 'upgrade' the language of the LXX in the first century BCE/CE is also apparent in some papyrus fragments (see above, Chapter 1, pp. 4–5) and throws an interesting light on the social and educational milieu of Jewish biblical scribes and scholars, sensitive to the literary fashions of their time. Other stylistic features include the use of synonyms and a preference for compound verbs. There is also an apparent concern to clarify the meaning and improve the grammar of the LXX by adding proper names, personal pronouns, conjunctions and so on. In the later stages, hexaplaric material is drawn on, especially Symmachus's stylish version, in order to preserve alternative readings through expansions and double renderings. In the historical books especially, there are editorial expansions of a theological, cultic or midrashic type. All this suggests that the texts were being revised primarily for inner-church use, in catechesis, preaching and so on. Despite claims to be more faithful to the Hebrew than the hexaplaric edition, 'correction' against the Hebrew is not a prominent feature (see Kamesar 1993: 35).

'Lucianic' or 'Antiochian' witnesses do not occur for all books of the LXX. So far, no trace of this type of revision has been detected in manuscripts of either the Pentateuch or the Psalms. This may be accidental, or it may suggest that, where the 'proto-Lucianic' revision is concerned, the books attributed to Moses (and David?) were regarded as having a different status from the rest, an attitude unlikely to have affected later Christian revisers; for the Psalms, liturgical use perhaps discouraged alterations. The Antiochian text is most strongly attested in the historical books and in the prophets.

What further complicates the issue is the probability that in some places the Antiochian text, already a valuable early witness, preserves earlier LXX readings than those in the standard manuscripts, though Fernández Marcos's claim that 'the Lucianic recension ... reproduces the ancient Septuagint with some stylistic corrections and a large number of additions taken from the Hexaplaric recension' (2000: 197) may be over-optimistic (Fernández Marcos is, however, one of the leading scholars in this area).

Much remains to be done to identify genuine Lucianic readings in marginal glosses and patristic writings; to distinguish between the third-century Lucianic recension as such and more loosely affiliated 'Antiochian' readings; above all, to sort out the 'proto-Lucianic' elements from those belonging to the later 'updating'. The incorporation of hexaplaric readings shows the reality of this later revision, which may well have been the work of the historical Lucian. The existence of 'proto-Lucianic' strata is witnessed by OL quotations in Tertullian and Cyprian; by remnants of the OL in some manuscripts of Samuel-Kings and the prophets; by the text sometimes used by Josephus in *Ant.* for the period covering Samuel to 1 Maccabees; and by an important Qumran text, 4Q51(4QSam^a).

Barthélemy proposed that 'proto-Lucian' belonged to the *kaige* group, but with a Graecizing as well as a Hebraizing character. This needs careful investigation: some scholars (Brock for instance, see Fernández Marcos 2000: 234) think that Barthélemy has oversimplified the evidence, discounting the clearly late features; while others doubt whether there are enough *kaige* features in Lucianic readings to justify the description at all. Tov in fact has suggested that the Lucianic text is so distinctive that it may represent a very early alternative translation (Fernández Marcos 2000: 235); the general presumption is, however, that we are dealing with a revision of the LXX. Until the picture is clearer, reconstructions of this tantalizing stage in the development of the LXX must remain tentative. As with the Jewish versions, the dividing line between translation and revision becomes less rather than more certain, as does the very identity of 'the LXX'.

Whatever the early history of the Lucianic witnesses – and even if it can never be fully brought into the light – Jerome was certainly right in pointing to a distinctive form in which the LXX was read and used in the Syrian churches centred on Antioch. It is easy to forget that all our manuscripts were produced within particular communities which had specific interests and needs. In this context, Fernández Marcos and other Spanish scholars have published a reconstructed text of Samuel-Kings-Chronicles as it would have existed in fourth-and fifth-century Antioch. This is a notable achievement, given the complexity and uncertainty of the textual evidence, and is a reminder that identifying the original form of the LXX is not the only task to be tackled (cf. Jobes and Silva 2000: 282).

Further reading

For discussion of the Jewish versions in general, see *ABD* 6, pp. 787–813, 'Versions, Ancient', especially Birdsall, 'Introductory Survey' (1992: 787–93) and Greenspoon, 'Greek Versions' (1992a: 793–4); Fernández Marcos (2000: 109–41); Grabbe (1992b: 505–56); Greenspoon (1990); Salvesen (1998: 135–398. This includes detailed essays on individual versions).

For the *kaige* tradition, the seminal work is Barthélemy (1963).

On Theodotion, see Fernández Marcos (2000: 142–54); Greenspoon (1992b: 447–8); Harl, Dorival and Munnich (1988: 150–7); Jellicoe (1968: 83–94); Jobes and Silva (2000: 41–2).

On Aquila, see especially Fernández Marcos (2000: 109–22; the most thorough recent discussion of the issues); Grabbe (1982: 527–36, on the differences between Aquila and the exegetical rules of R. Akiba); Greenspoon (1992c: 320–1); Harl, Dorival and Munnich (1988: 143–7); Jarick (1990: 131–9); Jellicoe (1968: 76–83; a detailed and helpful discussion); Jobes and Silva (2000: 38–40; a good brief survey of the main issues); Swete (1914: 31–42; a full presentation of sources, and examples of meaty passages of Aquila alongside the LXX, but in Greek only).

On Symmachus, see Fernández Marcos (2000: 123–41); Greenspoon (1992d: 251); Harl, Dorival and Munnich (1988: 148–50); Jellicoe (1968: 94–9); Jobes and Silva (2000: 40–1); Salvesen (1991).

On the Quinta and other minor versions, see Fernández Marcos (2000: 155–73); Harl, Dorival and Munnich (1988: 157–61); Howard (1974: 15–22); Olofsson (1997: 189–230).

For the Christian recensions in general, see Jellicoe (1968: 134–71); Jobes and Silva (2000: 46–8, 55–6, 304–7); Swete (1914: 59–86).

For recent thinking on the 'Hesychian Recension', see Fernández Marcos (2000: 239–46); Harl, Dorival and Munnich (1988: 172).

For Origen and the Hexapla, see Fernández Marcos (2000: 204–22); Harl, Dorival and Munnich (1988: 162–8); Jellicoe (1968: 100–33); Jobes and Silva (2000: 48–53); de Lange (1976; Origen's relations with the Jews); Norton (1997: 189–230); Parker (1992: 188–9); Salvesen (1998; a full coverage of the scholarly views); Wiles (1970: 454–61).

On the Antiochian Text/Lucianic Recension, see Fernández Marcos (2000: 223–38); Harl, Dorival and Munnich (1988: 168–71); Jobes and Silva (2000: 53–5).

CHAPTER 6

Language and Style

Introduction

The previous chapter has shown the complexity of the early history of the LXX as used by both Jews and Christians. This complexity throws into relief the massive task of the Göttingen editors, and others, who try to disentangle the manuscript tradition in order to establish, for each book, the earliest probable form of the text. This chapter considers another crucial area for establishing and understanding the text: the nature of the Greek used and the working methods employed by the translators.

For the books of the Hebrew canon there are texts for comparison, though in no case can we be certain that the translator's source-text was exactly the same as the MT; in some cases, Jeremiah for instance, it was evidently very different. For some of the apocryphal books, notably Sirach and Tobit, Hebrew or Aramaic exemplars have been at least partially recovered. For others, Judith for instance, or 1 Maccabees, a Semitic original seems likely, though none is extant. It is not always easy, however, to establish a book's style as being that of a translation from a Semitic original: Craven, for example, wonders whether Judith could not have been deliberately written 'in elegant hebraised Greek' (1983: 5). Other books, including 2, 3 and 4 Maccabees and the Wisdom of Solomon, were composed in Greek, in various different styles (for Wisdom, see Horbury 2001: 652; for Maccabees, Dimant 1987). When we talk about the Greek of

the LXX, we have to take into account these different
categories.

A broadly unifying feature is that both authors and
translators employ the 'Koine' or 'common' (i.e. 'shared')
Greek of the Hellenistic age. This ensures a certain homogeneity but, as with any body of literature produced over at
least two centuries, there are many variations in linguistic
usage and style. This is true even for the translated books,
where each translator has his own way of expressing his source-
text in Greek through lexical, grammatical and syntactic
choices, his own 'translation technique'. In this respect, it is
important to situate the LXX within current debates on
'vernacular' and 'literary' Koine, and to be aware that not all
contemporary writers define 'Koine' in the same way. The
importance of analysing each translator's 'technique', or style,
will also be discussed, and this will lead to an investigation of
whether translations express exegetical and theological ideas
different from those in the source-text and, if so, how. The
questions touched on in this chapter are fully and brilliantly
discussed by Fernández Marcos (2000: 3–31).

The Septuagint and Koine Greek

Koine differs in various respects from the earlier 'classical'
Greek associated principally with Attic, the form of the
language spoken and written in and around Athens. Ancient
Greece, geographically and historically, resisted unification,
and its language consisted of a number of distinct, though
related, dialects. For a while in the fifth century BCE, Athens
was dominant, both historically and culturally, and most
(though not all) of the literature equated with the great age of
classical Greece was written in Attic. During the period of the
Athenian Empire, and in its aftermath, Attic was widely used in
trade and other international relationships; in the process,
some of its distinctive features began to disappear, although,
in any case, there would have been differences between
everyday and literary speech. Elements from other Greek
dialects prevailed, archaic words and expressions, including

Homeric ones, reappeared. Some grammatical forms (the dual, for instance, and the optative) changed, simplified, and eventually all but vanished, in the normal way in which living languages evolve with time and circumstance.

Some changes appear already in the fourth-century writings of well-travelled Athenians like Xenophon and Aristotle. Then, in the wake of Alexander's conquests in the late-fourth century, this 'common' Greek became the *lingua franca* not only of the Mediterranean Basin and the Aegean, but also of much of the ancient Near East, including Egypt and Palestine. Greeks settled overseas in even greater numbers than before, and the common language not only facilitated trade and communication, but also helped to further Alexander's vision of a universal Greek culture. Even when the short-lived Empire broke up after Alexander's early death in 323 BCE, the Ptolemaic, Seleucid and Antigonid dynasties, between whom it was divided, were all of Macedonian Greek origin. So the linguistic situation did not change and Koine continued to be the expression of a cosmopolitan, multi-ethnic civilization.

Koine was also increasingly spoken by non-Greeks. At first, we may suppose, it was acquired as a second language for practical reasons, but before long it will have become the first language for many, including Jews. It is a language increasingly well known to us from inscriptions (decrees, dedications, memorials) and papyri (letters, documents), especially, in the latter case, from Egypt. It is also the language of much of the LXX (and later of the NT). Study of the inscriptions and papyri has shown how much the LXX reflects the common language.

Koine, whether in the Bible or elsewhere, must not, however, be equated simply with colloquial, vernacular language. It was also used in a more polished way (even some of the papyri and inscriptions display a consciously elegant style). In Egypt under the early Ptolemies, in the third and second centuries particularly, there was a new flowering of Greek thought and writing; it was centred on Alexandria, but other renowned cities like Athens, Pergamum and Cyrene were also involved. The result was a corpus of Hellenistic

Greek literature, both poetry and prose, which is now the object of increasingly appreciative study.

Among the writers of the second century BCE were a number of distinguished Jewish authors, who wrote in various genres. It is as part of this cultural flowering that we should probably understand some of the more 'literary' LXX translations (Proverbs, for instance, or Job). At the same time, the study, in Hellenistic schools, of earlier Greek literature showed up the differences in style with works written in Koine. From at least the first century BCE, there was a conscious move, in some literary circles, to revive the supposedly 'pure' Attic dialect used by the great authors of fifth-century Athens. There were also debates, extending into subsequent centuries, between proponents of Attic and those who defended the use of other forms of the language. This too has left its mark on the history of the LXX , where 'Atticizing' revisions occur from the time of the earliest extant remains as well as in the Lucianic Recension (see above, Chapter 5, p. 104).

In modern times too, the Greek of the LXX has been tried and found wanting. Swete is typical in calling it 'clumsy' (of the prologue to Sirach), 'a mongrel patois' (of the Greek spoken in Alexandria and perhaps reflected in the Pentateuch), and 'uncouth' (1914: 20, 292, 370). He appreciates the 'simple style' of the Pentateuch and the achievements of the authors of the Wisdom of Solomon and 2–4 Maccabees (1914: 312). Concerning the syntax of the translated books, however, he was so struck by the Semitic character, that he considered the LXX as not really Greek at all: 'the translators... are almost indifferent to idiom, and seem to have no sense of rhythm' (1914: 299). Many of these judgements, which were once widely accepted, are now being revised, though there is still much debate about the nature and extent of Semitic influence on the LXX's syntax. It is worth dwelling on the reactions of the older biblical scholars (classical scholars, on the whole, did not engage with the LXX) because they demonstrate how much their own cultural conditioning affected their responses. Immersed from their earliest years in a classical education, and taught to take the fifth-century BCE Greek authors as their benchmark, they could scarcely help being shocked by the LXX, a product of the Hellenistic age which itself was hardly thought worthy of study.

Their discomfort is not an exclusively modern phenomenon, as we have just seen in the matter of Atticizing. As well as the textual evidence for stylistic improvement, we also find Christian apologists already in antiquity defending the rough simplicity and old-fashioned language of the Bible (in Old and New Testaments alike) against the contempt of opponents with more sophisticated literary tastes. The third century CE was another moment of classical revival, within which must be set Origen's answer (*c.* 248 CE) to the earlier treatise of the non-Christian Celsus on *True Doctrine* (*c.* 180 CE). Celsus had sneered at the Apostles as a bunch of tax-collectors and sailors. Origen's reply defends the efficacy of their uneducated speech for preaching the gospel, along lines already used by Paul (possibly against a similar background; *Against Celsus* 1.62; cf. 1 Cor. 2.1–4?). There may be a hint of similar criticisms in the second-century CE apologist Theophilus of Antioch's comment that all the 'prophets' (that is, the biblical authors) were 'illiterate and shepherds and uneducated', *agrammatoi kai poimenes kai idiōtai* (*Ad Autolycum* 2.35; translation by Grant 1970). Swete suggested that Hellenistic Jewish writers deliberately paraphrased their biblical quotations in order to conceal the 'uncouth phraseology of the Greek Bible' (1914: 370), but this is unlikely. It is true that the preference for Attic forms over those of Koine affected vocabulary, verb endings and other features, as Pelletier has shown in the case of Josephus's updating of *Ep. Arist.* (1988: 106), but other apparent 'liberties' taken with the LXX have to be seen in the context of the normal way in which Greek (and Latin) authors deliberately disguised their sources (Spottorno has remarked on this in connection with Josephus, 1997: 382).

The Koine of the LXX is usually classed as colloquial or vernacular, as opposed to literary (though even Swete acknowledged in passing that there were some literary features present, and he forgets himself sufficiently to praise the LXX as 'a monument of early Hellenistic Greek'; 1914: 295, 340). This classification, although basically correct, needs to be modified by examining each book for its particular features. The line between non-literary and literary language is not as clear as has been assumed, which makes examining the LXX for stylistic features (these are briefly listed by Aitken 1999: 29) an interesting development.

In another debate, influential for some time, it was argued, from the supposedly high incidence of Semitic features thought to permeate the LXX, that there was a special kind of 'Jewish-Greek', not only the result of written translation, but actually spoken by Jewish diaspora communities, especially in Egypt (it was assumed, questionably, that Jews mainly continued to speak Aramaic in Palestine). This theory has been largely (though not entirely) abandoned. From the ever-growing body of secular papyri, as well as of Jewish inscriptions in Greek, it becomes increasingly clear that the language of the LXX is fundamentally the same as that spoken (or at least, written) elsewhere, particularly its vocabulary (Lee 1983; 2003; Horsley 1989). Furthermore, in Egypt the undeniably Semitic character of many LXX expressions and constructions has been paralleled in non-Jewish papyri, especially from rural areas. Rather than suppose Jewish influence on the local brand of Greek, it has been argued that a Semitic flavour has come into Greek from the local Egyptian (Coptic) dialects (Vergote in Fernández Marcos 2000: 10. Brock 1972: 33–4 notes that this was already remarked on by Lefort in 1928). Scholars are more inclined to speak now of 'translation Greek', rather than of 'Jewish' or 'synagogue' Greek, though, even here, it must be realized that much of the vocabulary and syntax of the LXX is not unusual and the term must not be used indiscriminately (Aitken 1999: 26). The translators were bilingual, and the effect of such bilingualism, in both directions, is an area of fruitful investigation (Fernández Marcos 2000: 9–12).

If the Greek of the LXX is to be understood as denoting 'a corpus not a language' (Aitken 1999: 30), there is still considerable disagreement as to how far Hebrew idiom has affected LXX Greek (so-called 'Hebrew interference'). Some (e.g. Swete 1914: 323; Lust in Lust, Eynikel and Hauspie 1992: viii–ix) thinks that Hebrew influence is all-pervasive, especially at the level of syntax. Others argue that, although the incidence ('frequency') of a few features is very marked, it is their repetition rather than their existence that creates the effect; the bulk of the LXX witnesses to a non-Semitized Greek (Evans 2001 argues this case with regard to verbal syntax in the Pentateuch). This is a controversial area, in which it is important that positions do not become polarized. Fernández Marcos has a prudent approach, following Rabin: 'in general it can be stated that the biblical Greek adopted by the translators of the Pentateuch became a sort of sub-language which later translators or the authors of pseudepigrapha, if they were bilingual, imitated' (2000: 24). Lust, although stressing Semitic features, admits that the LXX 'displays a great variety in style and vocabulary' (Lust, Eynikel and Hauspie 1992: ix). Abbott remarked on the significance of 'frequency' as early as 1891 (see Jobes and Silva 2000: 185).

The LXX is becoming increasingly valued as a witness to the literature of vernacular Hellenistic Greek. It constitutes the first oriental example of translation, a genre which became common only in the Roman period. Now that the Hellenistic age is no longer regarded as a kind of 'also-ran' in the study of Greek history and literature, reading the books of the LXX as Greek texts in their Hellenistic context can also appeal to readers and scholars beyond the disciplines of biblical studies. The LXX, in all the diversity of its individual parts and in whatever way its Greek usage is defined, belongs to, and emanates from, a flourishing Jewish culture, both in Palestine and the diaspora, which now finds its place within a wider body of literature.

The Septuagint's first readers

Even if the LXX can be studied as a corpus of Hellenistic Greek texts, it originated and developed within specifically religious Judaeo-Christian contexts, which have given it a distinctive character. LXX scholars are, however, divided about its primary purpose: was it designed to give its first readers access to the Hebrew texts, or was it to replace the Hebrew altogether; that is, how was it meant to be read?

Two modern approaches

The question is highlighted by the approaches of two major modern translation projects: the French-based Bible d'Alexandrie (BA) and the American-based New English Translation of the Septuagint (NETS). Each takes the language of the LXX seriously, and each has some problematic aspects.

(1) La Bible d'Alexandrie. The modern translators start from the conviction that the LXX is a collection of Greek texts intelligible as they stand. They have opted to translate each book in the way its first recipients might be assumed to have read it: first and foremost as a Hellenistic Greek text, understood without recourse to the Hebrew originals now beyond their reach (cf. Muraoka 2002a for the effects of this choice on lexicography; Jobes and Silva 2000: 261). How the texts were actually understood, if not from the very beginning, at least from not long afterwards, can be demonstrated from the writings of early Jewish and Christian authors who read their Scriptures in Greek.

There are two problems with this otherwise sound approach. One is that the earliest generations of readers, and their milieux, are largely unknown; there is a danger of equating them with the later Jewish and Christian writers who have left exegetical traces. The other is that the greater part of the LXX does consist of translations and, however much they may exist as autonomous works, they are marked by the form and content of their source-texts and invite comparison with them as an influence on translation.

(2) NETS. The NETS editors start from the opposite position. They insist that the LXX must be translated (and so accessed by modern readers) with the MT as chief 'control' because that is how the first translators worked. The translators' aim was to make the Hebrew text intelligible; the Greek translations were intended to be subservient to their Hebrew parent, a means to an end, and it was only later that they were read as texts in their own right (Pietersma 2001b: 219; Lust in Lust, Eynikel and Hauspie 1992: viii–xv discusses the implications for lexicography).

colophon) – we know nothing about their
characteristics are reconstructed from th
critical texts, on the assumption that the
the original translation (cf. Aejmelae
ison between the LXX and the M
equivalents, can show whether t
his presumed source, or ren
habitually handles Hebrew
tence (or not) he has i
what kind of lexical p
way, one translator
Study of trans
translator ma
source-text
exegetic
towar
dif

delicate operation, and one of great importance for modern
readers.

Translation technique

Each translator had his own methods, preferences and
peculiarities. Analysing these is an essential step towards
understanding not only how a translation works linguistically,
but also how the translator has understood and represented
the meaning of the original. This is what is meant by
'translation technique'.

Looked at from a slightly different angle, it may also be
understood as the way in which a text relates to its presumed
source. Conventionally, we speak of 'the translators', and of
course they existed; but – with the exception of Ben Sira's
grandson (and just possibly the person named in the Esther

identity. Their
e evidence of the
se are reliably close to
s 1991; 2001). Compar-
T, as at least approximate
he translator sticks closely to
ders it paraphrastically; how he
grammar and syntax; what compe-
either Hebrew or Greek (or both);
references he shows, and so on. In this
can be distinguished from another.
ation technique also indicates places where a
y have been interpreting or even altering his
It therefore has not only linguistic but also
l and hermeneutical implications, and can also help
s establishing date, place and cultural milieu for
erent translations.

There are, however, some problematic aspects to this area of study.

1. 'Translation technique' is a modern term which has become part of the jargon of LXX scholars. Analysing it is an increasingly scientific affair, especially with the aid of computers which can quickly cover large areas of text, show up patterns and produce statistics. The results are often impressive. Some of the implications, however, need to be considered carefully to avoid misconceptions. For one thing, 'technique' suggests something consciously chosen and systematic. It is unlikely that the early translators worked like this; their method is likely to have been *ad hoc*, experimental, not always consistent (Aejmelaeus 1991), as they grappled with the challenges and difficulties of a task for which there were at first no models. Rather than 'technique', or even 'method' (cf. Jobes and Silva 2000: 114–15), 'practice', or 'style' might be more appropriate. Admittedly, these terms are less precise, but they better suggest that the characteristics of a translator are what we, the modern readers, deduce

from any given text, even though the translator himself may have been unaware of them.

2. Even if the term 'translation technique' persists (as it surely will), the use of computer-generated evidence, being of its nature mechanical, must be handled with extreme care. Unless it is related to other features, especially context, it can produce too restricted a picture, especially where statistics from small text-samples are involved (cf. Wade 2000: 73 2003: 115–16).

3. Another difficulty is that translation technique works by analysing the relationship between the Greek of the LXX and the Hebrew which it represents. But we do not know for certain the exact nature of either the original translation or the original source-text. For much of the time, it seems clear that a text very close to the MT (certainly for the consonants, often for the vocalization also) lies behind the reconstructed text of what we accept as 'the LXX' (that is, the current critical editions). Close comparisons are accordingly made between the LXX and the MT to determine the translator's procedure and style. Where there are no divergences this may be safe, but as soon as there are discrepancies, the question arises whether the translator had a different reading in his source-text, whether he made a mistake, or whether he had some reason for making a deliberate change. The translator's normal practice may suggest one or other solution, but there is no way of knowing whether he has not, on this occasion, done something different. The use of the MT as default is unavoidable, but risky, given the plurality of forms in which Hebrew texts circulated at least until the end of the first century CE.

'Literal' and 'free' translations

The most widespread approach to translational style, system-atized by Barr (1979), is to identify it as either 'literal' or 'free' (see also Tov 1997: 17–29). By 'literal' is meant a close

approximation to the (supposed) source-text, word for word,
or phrase for phrase, and including grammatical and
syntactical idioms and word order; this is called 'formal
equivalence'. By 'free' is meant a style which is more
paraphrastic and idiomatic, and which apparently aims to
give the translator's understanding of the original rather than
to reproduce it quantitatively; this is called 'dynamic equivalence'. In both cases, the labels 'literal' and 'free' relate to the
MT, rather than to the Greek text as such; this creates a bias
which is not always helpful. Also, they suggest a polarity which
a number of scholars find undesirable. As the two translational
styles play a part in ideological discussions about the
translator's attitude to his source text, these reservations are
important.

Much work has already been done to classify and quantify
different books of the LXX under the two headings. In
practice, they are not exact terms. 'Free' is self-evidently an
imprecise description (which may include within itself
instances of 'literal' renderings), but even the apparently
more controllable 'literal' translation is open to different
nuances (no attempt at a truly literal translation is known until
Aquila; the apogee comes with a twelfth-century CE – or
perhaps earlier – interlinear rendering of Jonah which sticks to
Hebrew gender even when this clashes with Greek usage;
Brock 1972: 22; Fernández Marcos 2000: 177–8).

The books with the highest degree of formal equivalence
include Ruth, Ecclesiastes and Song of Songs, that is, those
associated with the Hebraizing *kaige* movement of the first
century BCE onwards, and which were probably (if our
manuscripts really preserve the original translations) among
the last to be translated. Psalms has often been classed as
extremely literal, but recent study suggests that this needs
modifying (see Schaper 1995: 31–3). Books exhibiting the
greatest degree of dynamic equivalence include Job, Proverbs,
Isaiah, Paraleipomenōn and LXX Daniel. Other books which
are usually classed as 'literal' rather than 'free' – including the
Pentateuch, the Minor Prophets and Jeremiah – demonstrate
the inadequacies of the terminology. While evidently closely
following a source-text very similar in its wording to the MT

(the source-text of Jeremiah was most likely quantitatively different), these translations are often idiomatic and innovative, even if in small ways. See, for instance, Gen. 2.3; 8.4; 8.7 (with the comments of Wevers 1993: 21, 102, 104); Amos 3.5; 3.11; 6.5 (with qualifications; see Dines 1992: 307–8). Harlé and Pralon list some of the lexical innovations of the Leviticus translator (1988: 24–5), while Bons, Joosten and Kessler consider the special features of the Hosea translator (2002: 35–43, 44–6).

Rather than think in terms of either 'literal' or 'free', it is probably better to envisage a continuum running from extremely literal to extremely free renderings, with many intermediate stages and combinations, on which the different translations, or even different parts of the same translation, can be located (cf. Barr 1979; Wright 1987). On this kind of sliding scale a good number of the books come out somewhere in the middle. Aejmelaeus's insistence that what we are talking about are features which modern scholars have spotted, analysed and organized into systems, rather than the deliberate intentions of the translators, is again to be stressed (1991: 27–8).

Identifying the translators
Translation technique is, however, an important means of identifying translators. Wevers (1991), for instance, has demonstrated that there were different translators for each of the books of the Pentateuch. Long before this, Thackeray discerned a single translator (or at least translational group) for the whole of the Minor Prophets; this translator was also responsible for large portions of Jeremiah and Ezekiel (1923: 28–39; much of this study, especially for the Minor Prophets, has stood the test of time). Tov (1976), however, working from a different hypothesis, has argued that LXX Jeremiah is the work of a single translator, which has been partially revised.

Distinctive and persistent vocabulary usage, where, for instance, the translator had a choice between synonyms, is often a good clue. For example, of two synonymous words for 'sword', the translator of the Minor Prophets prefers *romphaia*, while the Isaiah translator regularly chooses *machaira*; there are also clear demarcations, throughout the LXX, in the

ṣabaoth, (*kurios*) *tōn dunameōn* and *pantokratōr* for
wh) *ṣᵉbāôt*, between *Philistiim* and *allophuloi* for
...isunes', and so on. Such translational 'finger-printing' can
contribute to the broader perception of how closely, or not,
the translator is keeping to his source-text.

The underlying presumption is that translators are consistent in their lexical and syntactical usage and that inconsistencies indicate either a different translator or a corrupt
text. This assumption should be handled cautiously: too much
regularity may be a sign not of a translator but of an editor or
reviser. Inconsistency, it has been suggested, is the normal
outcome of a single translator working for a considerable
period of time and with a sizeable portion of text (see e.g.
Gooding for parts of Exodus, in Wade 2000: 55). Brock
remarks that inconsistency in the Pentateuch fits with the
novelty of the enterprise (1972: 32). Inconsistency in minor
stylistic features is, in fact, common experience. Common
sense suggests that ancient translators had similar aberrations.
It is perhaps a salutary thing to keep in mind when trying, for
instance, to allocate portions within a book to more than one
translator. Variations must be persistent and substantial to
count.

Style and context

There are two areas of particular relevance to assessing
translation technique. First, there is the phenomenon that
Evans calls 'stylistic flourishes' (2001: 263; see above, Chapter
3, p. 54). The presence of elements such as word-play,
repetition, chiasm, alliteration and so on, not strictly required
by the source-text, suggests that some translators, at least, had
an instinct for literary effect. This provokes serious questions
about translators' education and attitude to their cultural
milieu. Much careful work remains to be done in this area, but
it promises to be fruitful; we have already examined the
example of Amos 1.3–2.6 (above, Chapter 3, pp. 55–6).

Secondly, there is the phenomenon that Tov calls 'contextual
exegesis' (1997: 45–6). A sense of context is of far-reaching
significance for understanding how translators worked and how
they understood their texts. As with other features, there is much

variation between translators. 1 Kingdoms, for instance, is a mainly contextual translation (Taylor 1997: 2); the Leviticus translator 'loved to translate a recurring Hebrew collocation in various ways' (Wevers 1991: 56); while the translator of Numbers works from the immediate and not the wider context (Voitila 1997: 120–1). Contextual translation shows up when a rendering seems to be affected by the immediate surroundings (sometimes triggered by cultural or theological considerations, or by textual difficulties or obscurities). Examples occur in, for example, Gen. 6.11 (*adikia*, 'wrongdoing', for *ḥāmās*, 'violence'; see Wevers 1993: 82); Exod. 2.3 (the Egyptian word *thibis*, 'reed-basket', for *tēbâ*, 'container'; this contrasts with Gen. 6.14, where *tēbâ* is rendered by *kibotos*, 'container', 'ark'). Further examples may be found in Tov 1997: 46–7; Hiebert 2000: 85–8. A context from the translator's cultural setting may have influenced Exod. 22.27, where *theous*, 'gods', renders *'elōhîm*, whereas the immediate context requires 'judges'. Büchner suggests that the translator is making a gracious gesture to his polytheistic milieu (1997: 416–17); the rendering, however, could be understood as automatic rather than contextual. This example shows how difficult it can be to define a translator's intention.

Even more interesting are places where the translator makes intertextual connections. A striking example occurs in Genesis (not noted by Wevers 1993). In 1.2, the verb used of the movement of the divine *pneuma/rûᵃḥ* ('wind' or 'spirit') over the 'abyss' recurs in Gen. 7.18, of the *kibotos* (the Ark) during the Flood:

	LXX		MT	
1.2	(*pneuma*) . . . *epephereto*		(*rûᵃḥ*) . . . *mᵉraḥepet*	
		'bore onwards'		'was hovering (?)'
7.18	(*kibotos*) . . . *epephereto*		(*tēbâ*) . . . *hālak*	
		'bore onwards'		'went'

In neither place is the Greek verb (used of a raft being 'carried downstream' in Herodotus, *Histories* 2.96) an obvious choice for the Hebrew (for the possible exegetical implications, see Harl 1986: 87, 135).

A still wider intertextual connection is pointed out by Kreuzer (2001: 45), who shows how the translation of Deut. 26.5 may have been influenced by the narrative of Gen. 30–2. Deut. 26.5 reads 'my father was leaving Syria (*Surian apebalen ho patēr mou*)', whereas the MT has 'my father was a wandering (or "perishing") Aramaean (*'^arammî 'ōbēd 'ābî*)'. But according to the narratives in Gen. 30–2, Jacob is a man of substance on his way home from Aram (Syria). The translator of Deut. 26.5 has apparently adjusted his version to the Genesis narrative.

These examples (and many others could be added) suggest the making of deliberate connections between passages. Here, too, careful study is needed to identify this type of translational practice, which is also a form of exegesis, so as to better understand how the LXX can sometimes have interpretation built into its very fabric.

Attitudes towards source-texts

The kind of 'translational exegesis' just illustrated is relevant to the ongoing debate about translators' attitudes towards their sources. Certainly, the translators were Jews, translating into Greek their nation's holy books which, we may assume, possessed an aura of venerable tradition. The Mosaic books above all had become, with the help of those who expounded them, and through their use in worship, both a guide for life (*halakah*) and an authoritative history to shape views of past, present and future (*haggadah*). Early halakic and haggadic debates have left their marks on some translations (see e.g. Gooding 1976, on the 'miscellanies' in 3 Kingdoms; cf. above, Chapter 1, p. 17). Another factor to bear in mind is the diverse forms in which Hebrew texts were circulating in the third to first centuries BCE, and even later. Additions and rewritings were still affecting them. In many cases, even if the translators thought they were rendering the words of Moses himself (or David, or Solomon, or the various prophets), these were texts still in the making, still bearing the marks of development or even controversy (see Garbini 1988: 133–50 for one – controversial – theory about the late completion of the Pentateuch). For all we know, too, the translators may themselves have been co-shapers of the Hebrew scrolls studied and copied in their particular communities. And attitudes to the new genre of translation itself may have been very different from ours: 'what may appear as a translator's taking liberties with his text may have been quite appropriate to the expectations of the culture in which he worked' (Jobes and Silva 2000: 91–2). It may be relevant, too, to remember that at this time, in the translators' Greek educational culture, the almost-sacred Homeric texts were being intensively, critically and reverently studied.

This brings us to the question of 'canonicity' for the Hebrew texts. The translators' source-texts were certainly 'canonical' in the sense of being normative, authoritative and influential. During the period when most of the LXX was translated, however, it is anachronistic to think of them as 'canonical' in the modern sense of a fixed collection whose wording can be expounded but not changed. It is easy for later perceptions of the sacrosanctity of Scripture to be retrojected, but this should be resisted (cf. Harl 1993: 334). It is a tendency which has sometimes made debates about the translators' appreciation of the nature of their task unneccesarily heated.

The question is whether the translators felt free to adjust the consonantal text they had before them in the interests of their own exegetical and theological views, or whether their reverence for the text meant that they translated only what they found before them (or, in the case of a damaged or badly written scroll, what they thought they found). It is not really a choice between whether or not they held the texts to be 'holy writ' (cf. Orlinsky 1975), or at least it need not be presented in this way. What is at issue is how, for the translator, a living relationship with the sacred texts could be expressed. For the LXX scholar, it has to do, on the one hand, with making sense of the more literal forms of translation (why translate literally when paraphrases or rewritings were available as established genres?) and, on the other, of evaluating the significance of divergences of a potentially exegetical nature between the LXX and the MT.

Being able to describe a translator's normal practice is obviously important here, in order to eliminate what might look at first sight like an ideological change but which really

belongs to a particular way of handling the Hebrew. In Deut.
32.10 in the MT, for instance, God is said to have guarded
'Jacob' as 'the apple of his eye'. The LXX omits the personal
pronoun 'his', leaving the phrase indefinite. Some scholars
have taken this as evidence of an anti-anthropomorphic bias
on the part of the translator. It is, however, characteristic of
this translator to drop personal pronouns when the point of
reference is obvious, so the passage cannot be taken, on this
argument alone, to reveal a theological stance (Jobes and Silva
2000: 117; see further Chapter 7, p. 132).

Translation technique is also important for identifying
places where there really is a different focus from that of the
MT. In the latter situation a decision first has to be taken as to
whether the change is due to the translator and not already
present in the source-text, and then, if it is, whether the
change has been accidental or deliberate. To deny the
likelihood of deliberate changes a priori risks inappropriately
reading back into the time of the translators later Jewish and
Christian beliefs about the inviolability of the biblical text. We
do not have any external evidence for a reluctance on the part
of the translators, out of piety, to adjust the Hebrew text; the
internal evidence rather suggests the opposite. Philo, it may be
recalled, believed in the inspired nature of the Law of Moses,
even in its Greek form, but did not feel obliged to quote
exactly. The issue continues to divide scholars; on LXX
Genesis, for instance, Wevers (1993) and Rösel (1998) are
both convinced of the translators' active role, in contrast with
Hendel and Hanhart, who are more doubtful; see Brown
(1999).

Modern scholars sometimes give the impression that the
alternative to not altering the text of Scripture is promiscuous
tampering with it to promote personal views. It must, however,
be remembered that the translators were not operating in an
individualistic vacuum but as members of communities. These
communities will surely have spent much time pondering on,
debating and expounding their Scriptures. Many of the
apparent alterations of the Hebrew suggested by passages in
the LXX will have been the result either of already established
traditions, or of current 'rereadings', and not the invention of

the translators, let alone their whim. Even at the lexical level, where the first translations appear to have set the agenda for subsequent books, much of the technical vocabulary is likely to have been forged before the first translations were made, even though the LXX may provide the earliest written evidence (see e.g. Harl 1986: 55 for *diathēkē*, 'testament', as equivalent of *bᵉrît*, 'covenant'; other standard vocabulary may also have been established by 'the generations which preceded' the translation of the Torah, Tov 1999: 184).

On the other hand, some translational solutions to textual difficulties or to hitherto unnoticed halakic anomalies, may have been the translators' own responses to the text before them; these could then have influenced interpretation within the community. What must be stressed is the seriousness with which any exegetical changes will have been made; in fact, the translator will most probably have thought that his occasional manoeuvring of the text was in fact producing the correct meaning, especially where the Hebrew was obscure (Tov 1997: 169; cf. Aejmelaeus 1991: 25). Deviations from the source-text do not necessarily mean that the translator was not attempting to translate 'literally'.

The preceding discussion has assumed that, for whatever reason, the translator has been making a deliberate choice to be literal, because of the sacred nature of his text. But we should not, perhaps, press this too far. It is possible that translating 'literally' may not have resulted from so conscious a decision; it may simply have been the safest – and easiest – method for translators who were feeling their way into a strange new world. Formal equivalence is an obvious starting point for a translator, an 'easy technique' (Barr 1979: 50). If the practice of literal translation was experimental rather than ideological, it might help to explain why the translator of Genesis, supposing him to have been the first, exhibits right from the beginning of his work such a mixture of renderings, now mirroring the Hebrew exactly, now expressing the sense in accomplished and idiomatic Greek.

This brings us back to the question of what kind of text the translators thought they were translating and why they chose a particular approach. Aejmelaeus suggested, as we have seen (above, pp. 118–19), that such decisions may not have been thought out, or at least, we have no means of knowing what they had in mind (1991: 23–6). Brock, however, had earlier made a case for the translators' choosing between two models (1972: 17–20). The first model is that of word-for-word reproduction, such as existed for legal and administrative documents, where exactitude was essential. This kind of translation is known from Ptolemaic Egypt. Because the books attributed to Moses were regarded as a sacred law-code, Brock argues, the translators chose the method which would make it most accurately available. The second model is the literary one of reproducing the general sense of a text so as to make it palatable to readers in another language. The examples here, however, derive mainly from translations into Latin of Greek literary works (there is one Egyptian-Greek example, Brock 1972: 18–19). It is questionable whether the LXX translators made such a clear distinction, especially as the Pentateuch was not a legal document in the same way as those represented in the papyri (cf. above, Chapter 3, pp. 43–4). Added to this is the consideration, already mentioned, that not even the translation of the Pentateuch exhibits a purely or uniformly literal style. Translation technique, in any case, especially where it is categorized as 'literal' or 'free', should be distinguished from questions of ideology. If 'literal' translation is a sign of 'fidelity' to a sacred text, where does that leave the 'free' translator? Is he excluded from considering the text as sacred too? It is interesting that Cook (1995) finds the translator of Proverbs to be theologically 'conservative', however that may be defined (cf. further Cook 2001; Wade 2003: 227–32).

Conclusion

The work variously being done on the language of the LXX and on the translational styles and practices of the translators, shows how important it is for several different questions to be kept in view simultaneously. More needs to be done to locate the syntax, and especially the vocabulary, of the LXX's translated books within the whole corpus of Koine Greek, especially in papyri and inscriptions, and to compare the language of the books originally written in Greek with that of other Hellenistic authors. And the language itself needs to be related to the social and cultural context of those who used it.

The scope of translation technique needs to be broadened to include aspects of style and awareness of context. These are areas not easy to define and quantify, but they are important for creating a fuller and more nuanced picture of any text and of its relation to its presumed source-text. Some criticism has been voiced of the earlier, more narrowly 'scientific' approach in which textual phenomena are investigated without regard to their context (e.g. Schaper 1995: 21–2). But it is only possible now for scholars to work on both the linguistic and the semantic fronts because a great deal of necessary ground-work has paved the way for newer developments; neither approach can do without the other. Similarly, the opposite criticism – that some LXX scholars are being side-tracked from the more fundamental discipline of textual criticism by other kinds of even linguistic research, let alone by attempts to recover exegetical features, establish dating and so on – is too exclusivist (e.g. Pietersma 1985: 297; Jobes and Silva 2000: 276–7). Textual criticism is, of course, logically prior to all else, but it is unrealistic to think that there will ever be a stage at which all texts have been established and scholars can move to other concerns. Every branch of LXX study needs developing, and all disciplines need to contribute to, and learn from, one another (there are excellent observations here in Tov 1997: 11). The pluralistic character of the texts themselves requires a plurality of research out of which, by trial and error, a gradual increase in knowledge and understanding may emerge.

Further reading

On Koine Greek and related issues, besides items already noted, Fernández Marcos (2000: 3–17) includes an important discussion of bilingualism; Jellicoe (1968: 314–37) updates Swete (1914: 289–314; this still contains much useful detail, despite its perspective from the norms of classical Greek); Harl

(1986: 49–70) surveys lexical choices in LXX Genesis. See also Harl, Dorival and Munnich (1988: 223–66); Harlé and Pralon (1988: 47–51; on the originality of the LXX in relation to 'literary' Koine); Jobes and Silva (2000: 114–17, largely following Tov); Brixhe (1993); Horrocks (1997: 56–9; for the place of the LXX in the history of the Greek language).

On translation technique and related issues, Aitken (1999: 26–7) usefully contrasts the approaches of Tov and Schaper; Beck (2000) attempts to show how translators handle narrative. See also Fernández Marcos (2000: 18–31, especially 22–6); Harl, Dorival and Munnich (1988: 230–3); Jobes and Silva (2000: 86–102); Swete (1914: 315–41; to be handled with care because of some out-dated assumptions, but often illuminating and informative); de Troyer (1997: 326–43, a penetrating and original discussion); Tov and Wright (1985, a computer-generated assessment of 'literalness').

For BA and NETS, see 'Further reading' at the end of Chapter 7.

The Use of the Septuagint: from the Beginnings to the Present Day

It is obvious that the LXX differs from the MT in many respects. Do these differences mean that the LXX has a theological outlook distinct from that of the MT? What responses to the LXX can be detected in the earliest use made of the LXX by Jews and Christians? And why, apart from the needs of textual criticism, is it still worth while studying it as a text in its own right? These questions will be treated briefly in this final chapter.

Septuagint and Masoretic Text: interpreting the differences

Identifying distinctive theological elements

The LXX differs in many places from the MT: in word choice, in the order of verses or whole passages, in pluses and minuses both small and great, and in renderings that give a different sense from the Hebrew. What is not obvious is how to interpret the differences. Three approaches are worth considering.

1. A close comparison can be made between isolated verses where there are divergences, and conclusions drawn from them about the outlook of each passage. This can yield interesting results, but can be misleading if taken out of context.

131

2. More likely to yield sound results is the systematic exploration of a complete book, provided that all necessary areas are explored: textual criticism, translation technique, style and so on. Then one may get an idea of the theology of a particular book, which will not necessarily turn out to be the same as in another.

3. A third approach is to look at themes, in order to identify attitudes over wider areas of text. Early attempts to do this include studies of the anti-anthropomorphism thought to be characteristic of the whole LXX. More recent study has shown how misleading such generalizations can be if they are based only on soundings, and do not emerge from the kind of rigorous checks just mentioned. In the case of anti-anthropomorphism, wider investigation has shown that in fact the translators do not systematically avoid anthropomorphic descriptions of God (Jobes and Silva 2000: 95; cf. Chapter 6, p. 126). Similarly, theories about developments in the LXX in the areas of messianism, resurrection and so on, have to be treated with care. But if thematic investigations are carried out with sufficient rigour, interesting cross-textual patterns may emerge, as has been demonstrated for the theme of divine omniscience (Joosten 2000). The well-founded observation that the avoidance, in almost all contexts, of 'rock' as a divine title must be deliberate seems to hold good (Olofsson 1990; but NB contrast 2 Kdgms 22.2 with Ps. 17(18).3).

What is needed is a system of checks and balances whereby both types of investigation – by book and by theme – can be corroborated against each other; in other words, both methods are necessary and to be encouraged. The outcome of both, so far, is to show that there is no one 'theology' of the LXX, any more than there is of the Hebrew Bible; rather, there is an interplay of different 'voices', some more and some less distinct.

The difficult area of inner-Septuagintal interpretation – of where, and why, the translations preserve perspectives, ideas and theological viewpoints different from those of the MT –

has to be approached with great caution. Differences between Greek and Hebrew have to be shown to be really deliberate, and not part of the translator's normal way of handling vocabulary or syntax (though, as we saw in the last chapter, 'translation technique' is seldom a purely mechanical exercise, but part and parcel of the translator's way of understanding the text semantically). With this proviso, it is obvious that in many places the LXX witnesses to adjustments of various kinds that reflect the outlook of the translator and his milieu, whether or not these were deliberate. Even if it is unclear whether a divergence between the LXX and the MT comes from the translator or from his source-text, a difference of interpretation between the two texts has significance. If nothing else, it shows that there were different streams of tradition, and if the LXX witnesses to some elements in interpretation which have not otherwise been preserved in Hebrew, it is a very important window onto a period of biblical interpretation before the MT emerged as dominant.

Two examples demonstrate the part which an interest in interpretation may play, and the context in which such investigation needs to be done.

1. *Gen. 2.2.* The change here from 'seventh' to 'sixth' as the day on which God finished his work, makes it clear that God did no work on the Sabbath; this adjustment may already have existed in the translator's Hebrew scroll (made by whom, where and when?); or it may have been the result of halakic reaction to the traditional Hebrew within the translator's community; or it may have been an innovation by the translator himself. These uncertainties cause difficulties when the aim is to reconstruct the original text of either the LXX or the MT. But if the aim is to identify distinctive interpretations within the LXX that show up when a comparison is made with the MT, then interesting light may be shed on the exegetical (in this case, theological) concerns contained within the LXX itself, and which possibly point to the community that commissioned and used it.

2. *Amos 7.14.* Sometimes the translator was led by differences between Greek and Hebrew syntax to make a choice that, even if he was following his normal practice, may have involved prior exegetical decisions. In Amos 7.14, for example, the ambiguous Hebrew nominal clause, 'not a prophet I', *lō'-nābî' 'ānōkî*, is rendered in Greek as 'I was not a prophet', *ouk ēmēn prophētēs*, using a past tense, although a present would be equally possible from the point of view both of Hebrew usage and of context (Wolff 1977: 306; cf. Evans 2001: 86). The choice – which must be made by modern translators too – is significant for making sense of Amos's apologia and of the book's views on prophecy. But does it represent an exegetical or merely a linguistic decision? In the rest of the book, wherever the translator adds a finite verb in translating a nominal clause, he always observes sequence of tenses: when the aspect of the Hebrew main verb is open to past action, he uses the imperfect of *eimi* (2.8); where it is open to present or future, he uses the present (5.13, 18b; 7.2, 5; 9.7; and, significantly, 7.13). So, from the point of view of translational practice, the past tense in 7.14 merely matches 'and Amos replied', *kai apekrithē Amos.* It gives nothing away about the translator's own view, even though his rendering led to exegetical discussion later (see Dines 1992: 241–4). On the other hand, it is likely that such a key verse would have been debated and interpreted, so it is not unreasonable to think that the past tense also represents an exegetical decision (the choice of *eimi* instead of *ēmēn* following *apekrithē* would have been more obviously an exegetical choice over normal translational procedure; see Ziegler 1943: 199 for manuscripts which do in fact make this 'correction').

Modern commentators must therefore tread a tightrope in identifying and explaining interpretational material in the LXX. In any case, more often than not the LXX and the MT do not differ significantly, so that what the LXX 'means' appears to be the same as what the MT 'means', from the point of view of gaining insights into the attitudes of those responsible for the two texts. This needs to be kept in mind in modern exegesis of the LXX, where the temptation is to focus, in any given book, on the divergent material and to construct from that the beliefs of the translator and his world. But, 'passages that were translated literally ... are of equal importance as free paraphrases; both represent fragments of the religious notions of the translator' (Seeligmann 1948: 93). On the other hand, the LXX should not be read simply as the MT with aberrations; a sense different from that of the MT, in style and nuance if not in radical differences of thought, emerges from reading the Greek text as a whole, with all its minor variations.

Jewish and Christian reception history

Another approach to understanding the LXX is to look for interpretation in writings which use it, or depend on it. Interpretations may be of particular verses or passages or (mainly in Christian writings) of whole books. Through studying these, it is possible to begin assessing the contribution made by the LXX to the history of biblical interpretation, a contribution which is still much underexploited and under-valued. It is not possible, in such a short space, to do justice to this area of reception history, but a few pointers may be given.

The LXX took the place of the Hebrew Scriptures for Greek-speaking Jews in worship, study or private reflection. It was used by Christian writers too, whenever there was a need to call upon or expound the Jewish Scriptures which had been appropriated and absorbed as the Old Testament. Beyond the Judaeo-Christian matrix, and as yet little studied, Septuagintal echoes appear in popular semi-religious contexts like those of the magical papyri and of non-official inscriptions, and give a fascinating insight into a syncretistic hinterland where the Greek Scriptures circulated alongside other words of power (Fernández Marcos 2000: 267–8; Leonas 1999). There is an admiring reference to Gen. 1.3, 9–10 in the first-century (or possibly third-century) CE literary treatise *On the Sublime* by

Pseudo-Longinus (if the passage in 9.9 is authentic; it is treated as such by Dorival 1987: 19–20; text in Grube 1991: 14), and there are more disparaging assessments from other pagans, such as Celsus in the second century CE. But otherwise the LXX reveals its existence firmly within the range of early Jewish and Christian religious literature.

Early Jewish interpretation

The first hints of the Greek translations in use appear in the fragmentary remains of Hellenistic Jewish writers (Demetrius, Eupolemus, Aristobulus, and others), in *Ep. Arist.* and other pseudepigrapha, in the Apocrypha, and in Philo and Josephus. The use of Scripture by Philo and Josephus has been extensively studied, but the situation with regard to the Hellenistic Jewish authors who preceded them is more difficult to determine. Apart from *Ep. Arist.*, these writings have survived only fragmentarily, which makes a complete picture impossible. Also, as we have seen for Aristobulus (above, Chapter 2, pp. 33–4), they are found inserted into Clement's and Eusebius's borrowings from Alexander Polyhistor. This means that they have to be located within a double context: that of their own original concerns and that of the use made of them by the later Christian writers (mainly, here, to back up arguments about Greek dependence on the writings of Moses); and as the portions available depended on what Polyhistor included, there is really a third context to reckon with too. Little has been done specifically on the relationship of the fragments to the LXX (though Holladay 1983, 1995 has sporadic discussions). The main problem is that there are few straightforward quotations, the biblical references being mostly paraphrase or 'rewritten Bible' (cf. Chapter 4, p. 71). This often makes it difficult to know whether a given writer was referring to an actual Greek text, or whether he was alluding to ways in which biblical traditions circulated in general, presumably in Greek. A few examples will give an idea of this earliest Greek use of biblical material.

Hellenistic Jewish authors

Demetrius the Historian

Demetrius may have written during the reign of Ptolemy IV Philopator (221–204 BCE) or slightly later (Fernández Marcos 2000: 261). What little survives is quoted in Clement, *Stromateis* 1.21.141; Eusebius, *PE* 9.21, 29, perhaps also 19, although, *pace* Holladay (1983: 59, 62–3), it is not clear that this section (Fragment 1, covering Gen. 22) contains quotations. He apparently retells the 'national history in a form more acceptable to ... pagan neighbours' (Swete 1914: 370) and in the process alludes to the subject matter of Gen. 22; 35.16; 25.6; Exod. 15.23–25; Num. 11.34–12.1 (Holladay 1983: 62–91). The stories are told in very brief outline and the allusions are woven seamlessly into the narrative, without any exegetical comment. There is no sign of a distinction between the words of Scripture and the words of the historian. Scripture is absorbed and re-presented rather than quoted, yet there are sufficiently close echoes to show that a written Greek text was known to him; some wording is closer to the LXX than to the MT (Fernández Marcos 2000: 261). The nature of these allusions is typical of the way in which 'quotations' are handled in other Hellenistic writers.

Eupolemus

He belongs to the mid-second century BCE, if he is to be identified with the person mentioned in 1 Macc. 8.17; 2 Macc. 4.11 (Swete 1914: 370; Bartlett 1985: 57–8; Fernández Marcos 2000: 260). He is quoted by Clement, *Stromateis* 1.21, 130, 141; 1.23.153 and Eusebius, *PE* 9.17; 26.30–4, 39 (Holladay 1983: 112–56). The fragments belong to a sketch of Israel's history from Moses to Solomon, and focus particularly on prophecy and the building of the Temple. The claim to Jewish priority over Greek culture is made explicitly (*PE* 9.30). Although rewriting rather than quoting, it is clear that he is familiar with the Greek Pentateuch and with Joshua. It is less clear whether his account of Solomon's exchange of letters with Hiram depends on 2 Chron. 2.11–13. Swete assumes that it does (1914: 370), but Fernández Marcos doubts it (2000: 260);

Bartlett's useful introduction and commentary on selected passages does not include any discussion of Eupolemus's use of the LXX. The story-line is closer to 2 Chronicles than to 1 Kings, but there are details of language and content (the dimensions of the Temple, for instance) that do not fit either. The intriguing detail that Solomon was twelve years old at his accession does not occur in the MT, and in the LXX's textual tradition only in the reading of Alexandrinus at 3 Kgdms 2.12. In 1 Chron. 22.5, 29.1, however, he is called 'child' or 'youth', *paidarion/neos*; (MT has *na'ar* both times) and according to Josephus, he was fourteen (*Ant.* 8.2, 211; cf. Bartlett 1985: 64, 66). This detail seems to indicate that, as well as written versions, Eupolemus made use of popular traditions which also surface here and there in other passages. This is true of other biblical rewritings and is important to bear in mind when we try to envisage what, at this stage, constituted 'Scripture' and how it was used. In a fragment of Aristeas the Historian, for instance, quoted by Eusebius (*PE* 9.25), references to the end and the beginning of LXX Job have been inserted into an account of Genesis 36 (Job 42.17b–c; 1.1, 3, in that order). The additonal details about Job in LXX Job 42.17a–e testify to the existence of traditions which did not find their way into the MT. Pinpointing haggadic or midrashic material in the LXX, which sometimes surfaces only later in rabbinic literature, is an important contribution which LXX scholars can make to the history of biblical interpretation.

Apocrypha and pseudepigrapha

Apocrypha
The same situation exists as for the previous writers: where biblical material occurs, the text often needs establishing. Specific passages are sometimes discussed, or at least mentioned, in the course of modern commentaries, for example the citation of Amos 8.10 in Tob. 2.6, which differs from the LXX in all the extant versions and recensions (Otzen 2002: 22); similarly the adaptation of the same verse in 1 Macc. 9.41 (Bartlett 1998: 32), although Amos 8.10 itself may just be another version of a common saying. Occasionally modern

authors discuss the use of Scripture. Bartlett, for instance, deals with the 'attitude to Scripture' of the author of 1 Maccabees, though he does not consider whether the citations and allusions show any sign of reflecting translational adjustments where the LXX is used to represent the (presumed) original Hebrew (1998: 31–3). Coggins touches on the role of the LXX in Sirach's use of 'Scripture' (1998: 62–3).

In fact, the influence of the LXX may be more pervasive than just the provision of allusions or citations. Bartlett also notes that the Greek style of 1 Maccabees is that of 'the LXX', perhaps 'a deliberate attempt to associate the book with other writings accepted by the Jewish community' (1998: 19; cf. the supposedly 'Septuagintal' style of parts of Luke's Gospel; Johnson 1986: 201, 211; O'Fearghail 1989). The same may be true of *Ep. Arist.* and of Sirach; in the latter case, it has been observed that the translator adopts a 'Septuagintal' style quite different from the one he uses in his own prologue. This contrasts with the author of Wisdom, who knows the LXX but does not imitate its style (though see Horbury 2001: 652 for Semitic features). The question of what 'Septuagintal style' actually is needs addressing, given the LXX's lack of homogeneity; presumably, the more 'literal' features are what is meant.

Pseudepigrapha

Among the Greek pseudepigrapha, Sibylline Oracles 3 shows clear evidence of contact with the LXX. But here, as elsewhere, so much preliminary work is needed to define the relationship between biblical allusions and the text of the LXX that exegetical significance is difficult to establish (cf. Fernández Marcos 2000: 262). Swete gives several possible instances of contact, involving LXX Psalms and Isaiah (1914: 372). Charlesworth (1983; 1985) and Delamarter (2002) attempt to give full cross-references for the whole range of the pseudepigrapha; Charlesworth (2002: 3–4) discusses the nature of the citations, but without giving separate consideration to those in Greek. Bartlett's treatment again makes no mention of the LXX (1985: 35–55).

Philo and Josephus

The way in which these influential authors utilize their biblical material is too large and complex a field to deal with in detail here. The following paragraphs merely sketch their significance.

Philo

A list of Philo's exegetical works can be found in Swete (1914: 373). There is a brief discussion in Fernández Marcos (2000: 264–5, mainly concerned with the nature of the text) and a more extensive treatment in Borgen (1997; this discusses Philo's hermeneutical approaches and the different genres in which he expounds the Bible).

Philo continues the practice of earlier Hellenistic writers of paraphrasing biblical texts (e.g. *De Opificio Mundi*; *De Abrahamo*; *De Decalogo*). This 'rewriting' of the Bible is a genre also found in Hebrew (e.g. *Jubilees*, the *Genesis Apocryphon*). Philo also gives verse-by-verse expositions of biblical books (e.g. *Legum Allegoriae*; *Quaestiones in Genesin/Exodum*; *De Gigantibus*). These are in effect commentaries, with explicit citations of the text; again this genre is found in Hebrew writings (e.g. some of the *pesher* texts from Qumran). Sometimes the meaning of the text is explained directly; but the 'Questions and Answers' form constitutes a distinctive sub-division which enjoyed a great vogue in later Christian writing. It enabled Philo, and his Christian heirs, to tackle difficult or controversial passages (see below, p. 145).

The literary forms and the technical language of exegesis which Philo used to express his highly individual and profoundly Jewish thought were not his inventions: they owed much to the practices of Hellenistic Greek commentators on Homer and on Greek philosophic and religious works. Philo, however, developed these rather succinct treatments into complete commentaries (Fernández Marcos 2000: 275). To the scholarly conventions of his time Philo also partly owed his preferred method of exegesis. The allegorical approach to the meaning of texts, which he found particularly congenial, had been developed centuries earlier in attempts to interpret the Greek myths, mainly as found in Homer, in such a way as to make palatable otherwise morally unacceptable passages (especially those involving the bad behaviour of the Olympian gods), and to safeguard 'the authority and prestige' of the poems (Simonetti 1994: 5). As far back as the sixth century BCE, difficult passages had been explained in terms of natural or psychological phenomena, that is, allegorically. The method was developed particularly by the Stoics, from the third century BCE onwards, in philosophical contexts. 'At the beginning of the common era, this type of interpretation and its related terminology was widely used in scholarly circles and among people of literary and philosophical attainment' (Simonetti 1994: 6). Philo had, of course, Jewish predecessors who had made modest use of allegorical interpretations: Aristobulus and *Ep. Arist.* in particular. And Jewish tradition in the Hebrew Bible itself makes rudimentary use of this hermeneutical method in its various types of figurative writing (*mashal*).

In considering how the LXX is expounded by Philo, it is important to remember the scholarly origins of the allegorical and typological approaches to interpretation, with their intention to render hallowed texts comprehensible and morally acceptable to a later age. Philo had enormous influence on Christian writers like Origen and those associated with the so-called Alexandrian School. It is equally important to realize that Philo (and his successors) did not ignore literal or historical exegesis altogether. In fact, the simple designation 'literal' or 'allegorical' is usually too simplistic, and is certainly so for Philo (Borgen 1997: 284). But the identification of deeper meanings in the text beyond the obvious surface one, is certainly a marked feature of Philo's exegesis.

In all his exegetical work, Philo uses the LXX as his source. He considers the Pentateuch to have the same authority as the Hebrew version (cf. Chapter 4, p. 64), and there is no reason to think that he does not regard the other books as authoritative too, even though he makes less use of them. With Philo, we have for the first time a sustained interpretation of the LXX, including the places where it differs from the Hebrew, but this is a resource that awaits further study.

Josephus

With Josephus the situation is more complicated, because he
makes use of the Hebrew Bible as well as the LXX. His
Antiquities of the Jews belongs to the well-established genre of
'rewritten Bible', but there are direct citations as well as
paraphrases. Swete gives examples of places where there is
contact with the LXX (1914: 376–9). Compared with Philo,
Josephus prefers a more literal, down-to-earth type of exegesis.
This too had a long after-life; many Christian exegetes adopted
this approach (though in homilies, commentaries and 'question and answer' works, rather than in biblical paraphrases).
Josephus can be seen as an ancestor of the so-called
Antiochian School, with its emphasis on the plain sense of
the text and its sober style. The two 'schools' – Alexandrian
and Antiochian – are often juxtaposed. It is true that there was
antagonism and rivalry (and bitter doctrinal disagreements)
between different Christian churches, but this should not be
exaggerated: neither 'school' practised one form of exegesis
exclusively and many traditions were shared (Simonetti 1994:
67–8). Nor should Philo and Josephus be set up as rivals, with
Philo at the start of a diaspora-based, Alexandrian tradition
which then influenced Christian writers, and Josephus
representing a Palestinian, proto-rabbinic approach. There
was no absolute divide between diaspora and Palestinian ways
of using Scripture, as the Dead Sea Scrolls have shown, and
contacts were frequent at all times. What we have are two
individual styles and preferences, each of which is important
for understanding the part played by the LXX at the start of
the Common Era.

Early Christian interpretation

Influence of the Septuagint on New Testament interpretation

Apart from its significance as a witness to textual plurality in
the first century CE (see above, Chapter 5, p. 85), the NT is
important in several ways for its use of 'the LXX' (understood
as the whole range of textual forms in which the Greek
Scriptures appear there). It is clear that for all NT authors the

Greek texts constitute authentic and authoritative Scripture, and that for most of them they are their only source. It is striking that, despite the evidence within the NT of fierce controversy with various Jewish groups, the text-forms used are never an issue. This suggests that textual pluriformity became problematic only in the second century CE (see Ulrich 2000: 325). 'The LXX', in an NT context, refers therefore to a complex and non-homogeneous collection of sources.

As such, it provides proof-texts to back up arguments and in many instances it is reinterpreted to fit its new Christian usage. In particular, the Scriptures are all regarded as prophetic, and their contents are applied to the Christian story. As well as providing direct quotations and recognizable allusions, the LXX exercises a profound influence on vocabulary and style, though this varies from writer to writer and is not all-pervasive.

There are far-reaching implications to the realization that foundational Christian experience was articulated mainly in terms of the Greek biblical texts, and not directly the Hebrew ones. It is still normal to approach key theological ideas, such as covenant and redemption, by analysing the use of such terms in the MT. But it would be methodologically preferable to begin by examining the LXX and writings depending on it. Müller's 'plea' (1996) that the LXX should be used instead of the Hebrew Bible by Christians as the appropriate complement to the NT may be exaggerated, but it draws attention to important issues in the relationship between the NT authors and their biblical texts.

There are a number of up-to-date treatments both of the textual ramifications of NT quotations, and of the use made of the OT by NT writers; some are suggested at the end of this chapter. What will be briefly highlighted here is the distinctive effect that the LXX has sometimes had on NT authors in places where it differs from the MT. A few examples only can be given, but they demonstrate ways in which LXX readings provided NT authors with opportunities they would not have found in the Hebrew version alone.

1 *Isa. 6.9–10.* This difficult passage, which in the MT reads: 'make the mind of this people dull ...' etc., is rendered

by the LXX: 'for this people's heart has grown dull ...'
etc. The LXX perhaps avoids the scandal of God
apparently wishing to prevent the people's repentance.
In the closing words of Acts 28.27, Luke has Paul use this
verse to account for the non-belief of the Jewish leaders
in Rome and the justification of the Gentile mission. The
handling of Isa. 6.9–10 in the LXX and the NT is
discussed by Evans (1989: 61–8, 81–135).

2. *Amos 9.12*. The nationalistic promise of MT Amos 9.12 is
used in Acts 15.17 in its universalizing LXX form to
justify the inclusion of the Gentiles in the Church. It is
debatable whether this was the translator's intention (cf.
Jobes and Silva 2000: 195; Dines 1992: 302–4), or the
unwitting result of his (mis?)reading of the Hebrew (cf.
Joosten 2000: 36–7).

3. *Hab. 2.3*. In the MT, this verse speaks of the vision
(*ḥāzôn*, masculine) which will surely come (masculine
verb forms). In the LXX, a distinction is made between
the vision (*horasis*, feminine) and someone (*auton*,
masculine) who must be waited for, and who will surely
come (*erchomenos*, masculine). With the addition of a
definite article, Heb. 10.37 further pinpoints this
mysterious character as 'the one who is coming' (*ho
erchomenos*) and is able to relate the prophecy to Christ's
second coming.

4. *Gal. 3.15–18*. A different kind of possibility is provided by
the LXX's stereotypical use of *diathēkē*, 'will', 'testament',
for Hebrew *bᵉrît*, 'covenant', 'contract'. In Gal. 3.15–18,
Paul plays on the double meaning (the specialized
biblical one, and the normal Greek one): 'once a
person's will (*diathēkē*) has been ratified, no one adds
to it or annuls it [v. 15] ... My point is this, the law ...
does not annul a covenant (*diathēkē*) previously ratified
by God ... [v. 17]'.

Further examples may be found in Jobes and Silva (2000:
194–201); Dines (1990: 624).

Patristic use of the Septuagint

Exegetical use of the LXX continued beyond the NT and for as long as the LXX provided the main focus of attention, either directly in Greek or through the various versions, especially OL (see above, Chapter 1, pp. 9–11). Exposition of the Hebrew canon (and of the other books accepted by the Greek and Latin churches) played a central role from the very beginning.

As Christianity grew and diversified, the interpretation of key texts of Scripture became an issue both within Christianity (for instance, in controversies with Gnostics and other divergent individuals and groups who came to be regarded as heretics) and in encounters with Judaism. The part played by the interpretation of Scripture in all these controversies was crucial.

Polemical and apologetic writing, however, was only one aspect of the use of Scripture. The earliest evidence, from before the end of the first century CE, comes in pastoral contexts, with the letters of Clement of Rome and, in the early-second century, the Letter of Barnabas. A strongly pastoral and homiletic use of Scripture was to continue, marked particularly by typological interpretations, whereby key events, figures, objects and so on in the earlier Scriptures were seen as anticipations of analogous events in the life of Christ and the Church (the method, like allegory, has earlier roots; cf. 1 Cor. 10.4). There were also many expository works, using various literary genres, for the instruction and edification of the faithful; brief summaries of books (*kephalaia*); full-scale commentaries; collections of 'Questions and Answers' on difficult passages; anthologies of thematic texts (*florilegia*), sometimes with extracts from commentaries added (*catenae*); and various others.

Early Christian writers followed certain basic principles. When the NT writings were definitively collected, both they and the earlier Scriptures were regarded as one unified corpus. The NT, however, was the point of departure for understanding the OT, and in instances of textual discordance the NT was always given precedence. For example, both the

LXX and the MT of Amos 5.27 read: 'I will take you into exile *beyond Damascus.*' The NT, however, in Acts 7.43 has 'beyond *Babylon*' (emphases added). Although patently odd, this reading is upheld as correct, simply because it is in the NT and 'the first martyr could not have made a mistake' (Jerome, *In Amos*; for this and the remarks of other patristic writers, see Dines 1992: 173–4).

The OT was mainly understood as the story of God's preparation of the people who would receive Christ; all the Scriptures were regarded as divinely inspired and so prophetic. The prophetic nature of Scripture contributed to the belief that, as well as a literal meaning, there were also moral, typological and allegorical ones, and always, within every passage, a spiritual meaning and application which included the others (de Lange 1976: 83). Where writers differ is in their choice of method, in the emphasis they give to the literal meaning (which includes textual discussion), the typological meaning and the allegorical meaning (which often involves etymologizing), and in the combination of these different strands of interpretation. Origen, for instance, considered that the literal sense was for simple folk who could not follow explanations of a more demanding kind, while the real treasures of Scripture were to be found only through the more spiritual forms of exegesis. The Antiochian exegete Theodore of Mopsuestia, on the contrary, insisted that the first meaning of the OT lay within the history of Israel itself; he only allowed a very few verses to have a christological extension, although he acknowledged the typological sense of all the OT (Simonetti 1994: 69–74). Many authors, both Alexandrian and Antiochian, engaged in both kinds of exegesis, though usually emphasizing one over the other. Theodoret of Cyrrhus, for instance, although an Antiochian exegete, has a taste for allegory (Simonetti 1994: 74–6; Siquans 2002). Jerome, uniquely, attaches the literal, historical meaning to the Hebrew text, and the spiritual meaning(s) to the traditional LXX (Dines 1992: 23–4; 1998: 425).

The influence of the Septuagint on biblical interpretation

The nature and scope of patristic use of the Bible has been treated in several standard works (see 'Further reading'); as with the NT, I will simply give here a few examples of places where lexical choices, or material special to the LXX, have played a significant part in interpretation.

1. *Isa. 7.14.* For texts crucial to Jewish-Christian controversy, Isa. 7.14 is one of the most obvious candidates. Here, the LXX's choice of *parthenos*, 'virgin', to render Hebrew *'almâ*, 'young woman', seemed to prove the miraculous nature of Christ's birth (it had already been used in Matt. 1.23). Jewish exegetes used versions with more neutral Greek renderings, such as *neanis* ('the Three'). Debates of this kind were instrumental in showing Christians that there were differences between the Hebrew and Greek texts and, even if they stuck staunchly to the LXX as inerrant, it was a contributing factor in the attempts of Origen and others to apply more rigorous checks on the text. What prompted the original choice of *parthenos* by the Isaiah translator in the mid-second century BCE is impossible to tell; he may have drawn on existing Jewish exegetical tradition (Fernández Marcos 2000: 172, n. 81), or he may simply have wished to indicate that the girl was a virgin when she conceived.

2. *Prov. 8.22.* In this case, the lexical choice affected interpretation in an inner-Christian controversy. To describe the relationship of wisdom to God in creation, the MT uses an ambiguous verb, *qānan*, 'created' or 'acquired' or 'begot'; the LXX uses a creation verb, *ktizō*. Whatever the implications in the original translation, the text in Christian usage seemed to say clearly that divine Wisdom (now identified with Christ) had been created, not begotten. In the debates with Arius in the fourth and early-fifth centuries over the nature of the Son, this verse was used as a proof-text by those who argued for the subordinate status of the Son, while those who maintained that he was 'begotten' not 'created' had to

be able to handle this Greek verse (the Hebrew would have left the argument open). For more on this controversy, see Simonetti 1994: 127–8.

3. *Amos 4.13.* The same verb played a part in the slightly later controversy over the status of the Holy Spirit. A key text here was Amos 4.13. The MT reads: 'For see, the one who ... creates wind (*bōrē' rûᵃḥ*), reveals his thoughts (*mah-śēḥô*) to mortals ...'. The LXX has, 'For see, I am he who ... creates wind (*ktizōn pneuma*) and proclaims to men his anointed (*christon autou*)...' The apparently clear reference to the second Person of the Trinity with *christon* (the translation presupposes a different division and vocalization of almost the same Hebrew consonants read more plausibly by the MT) made it natural to take *pneuma* as referring to the Holy Spirit. Unfortunately, the sense seemed to be that the Holy Sprit was a creature. The verse figured prominently in disputes about the consubstantiality of the Spirit, even after the definition of the Council of Constantinople in 381 CE, until eventually contact with the Hebrew text made it clear that there was no reference to Christ there and that *pneuma* probably had its ordinary meaning of 'wind'. As with Isa. 7.14, it is difficult to know how to interpret the exegetical import of the original translation, which can be explained in terms of a misreading of the Hebrew consonantal text, but which may perhaps also be the outcome of contemporary eschatological interpretation. For further discussion, see Dines (1992: 152–6).

4. *Job 42.14.* A very different problem was encountered here, where the name of Job's third daughter, in Hebrew *keren-happûk*, 'horn of antimony' (or, 'pot of eye make-up'), is rendered as *Amaltheiās keras*, 'horn of Amaltheia' (the 'horn of plenty', associated in Greek mythology with the nymph who fed the infant Jupiter on goat's milk). Theodore of Mopsuestia was so shocked by this rendering that he concluded (on other grounds as well) that the author of Job must have been a pagan. For more

details on this, and for other examples, see Dines (1990: 624).

Issues in the patristic use of the Septuagint

If the above examples seem rather desultory, it is because, in this area, 'the history of Christian exegesis has yet to be written' (Fernández Marcos 2000: 280). The amount of raw material waiting to be studied is vast and specialized. It needs, as Harl has said, co-operation between LXX scholars and patristic experts (1999: 193; she, of course, combines both areas of expertise). But there are difficulties to be overcome. Critical editions are needed for a great many patristic works before reliable translations can be made from the Greek or Latin. One of the major obstacles in the way of this essential work is that establishing the text of the LXX used by any given author is often difficult: as for the Hellenistic Jewish authors, decisions must be taken about whether a passage is being paraphrased or quoted directly. In the latter case, the citation must be identified textually: is it a witness to the oldest form of the LXX? Or has it been affected by one of the recensions (Hexaplaric, Antiochian, etc.)? Or even 'normalized' against reworkings in the NT? This is a slow process, and it is understandable that some scholars are reluctant to utilize patristic evidence until the textual work has been accomplished. But Fernández Marcos is surely right to insist that '[i]t is absolutely necessary to work on two fronts: by the production of modern critical editions that will reduce the great textual anarchy present in the field, and by monographs that trace the history of exegesis through the various schools and writers' (2000: 285); Siquans (2002), on Theodoret of Cyrrhus, provides one contribution. There are a number of reasons why this gargantuan task is so necessary.

1. The patristic writers reveal the effect of the LXX on the development of Christian thought during its first momentous centuries; to ignore or pass superficially over this period is to lose out on a whole rich world of biblical interpretation and risk having an impoverished

understanding of some of the deepest roots that have fed into the modern world.

2. The writers of the first four to five hundred years CE were closer to the language and culture of the LXX itself than we are, despite the linguistic and historical changes that occurred as time passed and the Hellenistic Age passed into that of first the Roman and then the Byzantine Empire. The Christian writers who used the Greek Bible were, in the main, still Greek speakers themselves; Harl has made a case for taking more seriously than is often done their reactions to unusual or problematic words, or to readings which may be authentic but which are passed over by modern editors (1999: 196–200; cf. Leonas 2001: 393). Fernández Marcos, too, draws attention to the importance of patristic evidence, which is not always fully exploited in the Göttingen editions (2000: 258–9). As many scholars confidently assert that these editions are reliable reconstructions of the earliest form of the LXX, it is important to be aware of this proviso. The editors may understandably feel that the patristic evidence is not yet sufficiently under control, but, as more reliable patristic texts become available, occasional adjustments to their reconstruction of 'the LXX' may well become necessary.

3. The complete patristic commentaries show how whole books were understood in Greek by Greek-speaking exegetes (a prologue often indicates the author's grasp of the main argument, aim and continuity of a biblical book). Often, too, the arrangement into sections is of interest in showing how the text was understood long before the later Hebrew-based divisions. Comparisons between different commentaries on the same book (for instance, those of Theodore of Mopsuestia, Theodoret of Cyrrhus and Cyril of Alexandria on the Minor Prophets, all written in the fourth or fifth century) point up exegetical differences, similarities, borrowings, shared traditions and other elements that shed light on the way the LXX functioned in the life of different churches.

This does not mean that everything in patristic writings is useful (cf. Harl 1999: 200; Fernández Marcos 2001: 239–40). These writings do show, however, that, provided we understand their hermeneutical and exegetical principles and methods, they have a serious contribution to make, both textually and for the history of interpretation. Despite the challenges they present, they should not (*pace* Jobes and Silva 2000: 204) be 'beyond the scope' of any new general survey of the LXX's history and influence.

Modern interest in the LXX

Today, LXX studies are flourishing, and on a number of fronts: textual, linguistic, exegetical and cultural (for a brief resumé of great clarity, see Harl 1988).

The Septuagint and textual criticism

Work continues, and will necessarily always continue, to establish as reliable a text of the LXX as possible, through assessing manuscript evidence, including any new material that may become available (papyri, inscriptions, etc.) and through evaluating readings both in other versions (OL, Coptic, etc.) and in secondary sources (e.g. patristic writings). Although we can never be completely certain that the earliest form of the translations has been recovered, we need to have the kind of thorough and reliable editions that the Göttingen editors provide. All other work depends on having a wide range of textual witnesses easily available through the critical apparatuses, so as to see where a given text has a simple history, and where there are complications or uncertainties.

The first task, then, is to establish the text of the LXX itself. But for some scholars the ultimate interest is the Hebrew Bible, and the LXX is studied as a potential aid to the textual criticism of the MT (e.g. Klein 1974; Tov 1997). This means assessing whether the Hebrew lying behind divergent readings of the LXX differed from the MT and, if so, whether it can be reconstructed by retranslating the LXX into Hebrew (retroversion). Translation technique and the other factors which might explain a divergent reading without positing a different source-text have, of course, to be considered. Evidence from the Dead Sea Scrolls has, in some cases, proved that the LXX's source-text was indeed different (e.g. for Jeremiah, Job and 1–2 Kingdoms, where the differences are substantial; for Amos 1.3 and Gen 1.9, to mention just two minor examples). These finds make it credible that other divergences stem from the translators' scrolls, rather than their exegesis (though this is usually disputable) and that these too may contribute to the task of reconstructing forms of pre-Masoretic Hebrew. The textual critic then has to decide whether non-Masoretic readings in the LXX are witnesses to some alternative Hebrew version, or whether they preserve a more authentic reading against which the MT should be corrected. The presupposition here is that there was one original Hebrew form of each book which then gave rise to different 'recensions' (i.e. an *Urtext* model similar to that assumed for the LXX; cf. above, Chapter 3, pp, 58–9). Tov (1997) sets out the criteria and explores the evidence in a masterly way. This utilization of the LXX is entirely proper, although it belongs to the study of the Hebrew rather than the Greek Bible. It is only undesirable if it gives the impression that somehow the Hebrew Bible is more important *per se* than the Greek one, whereas, for reasons both textual, religious and cultural, the LXX has its own intrinsic value as an object of study.

Modern translations

There is an urgent need for good up-to-date translations into modern languages; happily, a number of projects are under way, of which only a few can be mentioned here. The French-based Bible d'Alexandrie (BA) and the American-based New English Translation of the Septuagint (NETS) are among the most important and have already been discussed in Chapter 6 (above, pp. 116–17). A new German translation is also under production, nearer to NETS in its approach than to BA, but drawing on the insights of both (Kreuzer 2001), and there are other projects in, for instance, Spain and Italy . All these, but especially NETS and BA, point up different approaches to understanding the LXX, its relation to its source-text and to its Greek readers, and the way in which a modern translation should reflect this relationship.

Harl defines the aim of the BA as 'to offer as exact a translation of the Greek text of the LXX as possible' (2001: 181). The text is to be translated as a Hellenistic Jewish reader, and as a later Christian one, would have understood its Greek; the sense of the Hebrew original is not to be imposed on it. On the other hand, as the BA aims to give modern French readers a chance to encounter the LXX in the way in which it was first received, that is, as Scripture, some traditional vocabulary is retained (such as *seigneur* for *kurios* and *alliance* for *diathēkē*), a deliberately archaic style is sometimes sought and adjustments are made to what would otherwise sound too shockingly literal in French (Harl 1998: 35; 2001: 196–7). As the emphasis is on the early reception of the LXX as Scripture, coverage is given, through exegetical notes, to Jewish and (especially) Christian interpretation. For an evaluation and critique, see Fernández Marcos (2001: 238–40).

The goal of NETS is to create both 'a faithful translation of the LXX' and 'a tool for synoptic use with the NRSV for the study of the Greek and Hebrew Bible texts' (Pietersma 2001b: 217). The focus is on the relationship between the LXX and its Hebrew (and occasionally Aramaic) sources. The fundamental conviction is that the Greek versions were solely intended to render the Hebrew accessible. They were so influenced by Hebrew language and constructions that a modern translator is justified in rendering the Greek according to the meaning of the Hebrew, since this is what the translator intended (cf. above, Chapter 3, p. 52; Chapter 6, p. 116). For illuminating evaluation and critique, see van der Kooij (2001: 229–31) and Fernández Marcos (2001: 233–8).

It will be disastrous if the two approaches become entrenched positions. It is true that they reflect two radically different perceptions of the origins of the LXX (neither of them verifiable for the moment) and of its nature as a text, but they also have much in common. Both take the Greek text seriously and aim to render it faithfully (they part company on modern translational method). And both give necessary help

to modern readers who cannot manage the original Greek or
Hebrew. Neither is without its problematic aspects: for NETS,
the adjusting of the LXX to the NRSV, that is, essentially to the
MT; for BA, the filtering of the LXX through 'readers' who
belong to different times and places. Fernández Marcos
suggests that we also need, for 'a biblically well-educated
audience', a modern translation of the LXX as free-standing
Jewish Hellenistic literature, which would prioritize neither
Hebrew source-texts nor later reception (2001: 236–7). But
even this neutral approach would not solve the problem of a
necessary historical context in which to ground a translation,
the missing Archimedean point for LXX origins.

The Septuagint as Christian Scripture

There is a growing appreciation in Christian biblical studies of
the importance of the LXX for the NT, the Apocrypha and the
early interpretation of the Hebrew Bible. It is also appreciated
as a constituent element in patristic study and in the early
history of biblical interpretation in both eastern and western
churches. For some, there is also a hermeneutical interest in
how to present and use the LXX in the context of
contemporary church life and Bible study. Commentaries on
individual books of the LXX are now a desideratum, as well as
more monographs and specific studies.

The Septuagint as Jewish Scripture

The rediscovery of the LXX as the medium in which many
Hellenistic (and later) Jews, both in Palestine and elsewhere,
heard, read and knew the Law and the Prophets and the other
books of their ancestors (cf. the prologue to Sirach), is proving
fruitful for research. The LXX takes us back before the
Christian era to the Jewish culture which gave it birth. The
study of the LXX as a witness to the religious outlook of Greek-
speaking Judaism (in which already elements of later rabbinic
halakah and *haggadah* can be discerned) is one which
encourages the reconstruction of the historical circumstances
(including date and place) of the translations themselves. To
talk of 'the LXX' (in the sense of the modern edited texts) as

'the Bible of Hellenistic Judaism' could, however, be misleading. Evidence is accruing of how quickly alternative versions began to circulate, whether accidentally altered or deliberately revised or 'corrected'. The existence of the latter category shows that 'the LXX' (in the sense of the original translations) was never universally accepted. It would be more accurate to talk about 'the Bible in Greek' (just as 'the LXX' as 'the Bible of the Early Church' needs to be analysed into the various text-forms and recensions used in the different churches).

The Septuagint and Hellenistic culture

One of the most promising new developments in LXX study is the interest shown in it by classical scholars and historians of the Hellenistic period. This accompanies a marked surge of interest in Hellenistic language, literature and culture in general. The older perception of the LXX as the Hebrew Bible rendered into a Greek which is clumsy (or worse) and heavily permeated by Semitisms, is changing as study of the language of the LXX goes hand in hand with a better understanding of Koine Greek itself. Clearer definitions of how to distinguish Semitisms from natural Greek usage suggest to some linguists that the LXX could be an important witness to a crucial period (the third and second centuries BCE) in the development of Koine. But there is urgent need for critical tools: a complete grammar and a full lexicon of the LXX being two of the most obvious lacks (but see Boyd-Taylor 2001 for problems in lexicography due to lack of agreement – highlighted by the BA and NETS approaches – on the very nature of the Greek to be translated).

As literature, too, the LXX deserves examination and appreciation alongside the other remains of what was manifestly a time of brilliance and productivity for Jewish writers. Greater co-operation between biblical and classical scholars could result in exciting new insights on both sides. For as well as marking the beginning of a new phase in Judaism, with the traditional Hebrew Scriptures rendered into a new language, the LXX is, as far as we know, a new genre in Hellenistic Greek literature, the first sustained attempt to render the religious texts of a Semitic people into Greek: not just paraphrasing the essentials, as some of the other educated Jewish writers did, but representing them word by word, book by book, mostly in the common idiomatic language of everyday life, occasionally in something more obviously literary.

From whatever perspective we approach it, the LXX is surely an achievement which invites surprise, admiration and continuing study on all fronts.

Further reading

Much of the content of this chapter is covered by Fernández Marcos (2000, Chapters 17 ('Indirect Transmission: Biblical Quotations') and 20 ('The Religion of the Septuagint and Hellenism'); Jobes and Silva (2000, Chapters 10 ('Interpreting the Septuagint') and 14 ('Theological Development in the Hellenistic Age'). See also Dines (1990); Joosten (2000).

For more on Hellenistic Jewish authors and pseudepigrapha, see Swete (1914: 369–72); Harl, Dorival and Munnich (1988: 269–72); Holladay (1983); Bartlett (1985: 35–55 ('the Sibylline Oracles'), 56–71; ('Eupolemus') van der Horst (1988).

For Philo, see Borgen (1992: 337–9; 1997, Chapters 3–7; on the various exegetical forms used by Philo); Kamesar (2002). For Josephus, see Bartlett (1985: 79–86, on *Ant.*); Feldman (1992: 985–8); Pelletier (1988: 99–102).

For the New Testament, see Fernández Marcos (2000: 320–37); Harl, Dorival and Munnich (1988: 274–88); Jobes and Silva (2000: 183–205); Swete (1914: 381–405 ('Quotations from the LXX in the New Testament'); Longenecker (1975); McLay (2003).

On the Early Church, see Fernández Marcos (2000: 274–86 ('*Aporiae* and Biblical Commentaries'), 287–301 ('The Literature of the *Catenae*'), 338–62 ('The Septuagint and Early Christian Literature'); Harl, Dorival and Munnich (1988: 289–320); Swete (1914: 406–32 ('Quotations from the LXX in Early Christian Writings'), 462–77 ('Influence of the LXX on

Christian Literature'); Harl (1999); Horbury (1988: 727–87); Simonetti (1994).

For the BA/NETS approaches to translation, see Harl (2001: 181–97); Pietersma (2001b: 217–28), with the evaluations of van der Kooij (2001: 229–31) and Fernández Marcos (2001: 235–40). Hiebert (2001: 263–84) gives a 'hands-on' demonstration of the NETS method for Genesis; Dogniez (2001: 199–216) does the same for BA Zephaniah. The NETS website (which includes a general introduction to the project) may be found at http://ccat.sas.upenn.edu/nets/. See also Pietersma 1996 for the NETS translators' handbook. For details about BA, go to http://www.tradere.org/biblio/lxx/harl.htm. The website for the new German translation-project is found at http://www.uni-koblenz.de/~sept/index2.html.

Bibliography

Ackroyd, P., and C. Evans (eds) (1970) *The Cambridge History of the Bible, 1. From the Beginnings to Jerome* (Cambridge: Cambridge University Press).

Aejmelaeus, Anneli (1991) 'Translation Technique and the Intention of the Translator', in Cox 1991: 23–36.

(2001) 'What We Talk about When We Talk about Translation Technique', in Taylor 2001: 531–2.

Aejmelaeus, Anneli, and Udo Quast (eds) (2000) *Der Septuaginta-Psalter und seine Tochterübersetzungen* (MSU 24; Göttingen: Vandenhoeck and Ruprecht).

Aitken, James K. (1999) 'The Language of the Septuagint: Recent Theories, Future Prospects', *BJGS* 24: 24–33.

Amir, Y. (1988) 'Authority and Interpretation of Scripture in the Writings of Philo', in Mulder 1988: 421–53.

Austermann, Frank (2000) 'Thesen zur Septuaginta-Exegese am Beispiel der Untersuchung des Septuaginta-Psalters', in Aejmelaeus and Quast 2000: 380–6.

Barclay, John M. G. (1996) *Jews in the Mediterranean Diaspora: From Alexander to Trajan (323 BCE–117 CE)* (Edinburgh: T. & T. Clark).

Barr, James (1979) *The Typology of Literalism in Ancient Biblical Translations* (MSU 15; Göttingen: Vandenhoeck and Ruprecht).

Barthélemy, Dominique (1963) *Les Devanciers d'Aquila* (VT Sup 10; Leiden: Brill).

(1974) 'Pourquoi la Torah a-t-elle été traduite en grec?', in Black and Smalley 1974: 23–41.

Bartlett, John (1973) *The First and Second Books of the Maccabees* (Cambridge: Cambridge University Press).

— (1985) *Jews in the Hellenistic World. 1.1. Josephus, Aristeas, the Sibylline Oracles, Eupolemus* (Cambridge: Cambridge University Press).

— (1998) *1 Maccabees* (Sheffield: Sheffield Academic Press).

Barton, John, and John Muddiman (eds) (2001) *The Oxford Bible Commentary* (Oxford: Oxford University Press).

Beck, John A. (2000) *Translators as Storytellers: A Study in Septuagint Translation Technique* (New York, Oxford: Peter Lang).

Bettenson, Henry (1972) *Augustine, City of God* (Harmondsworth: Penguin Books).

Bickerman, Elias (1959) 'The Septuagint as a Translation', *PAAJR* 28: 1–39 (reprinted in *Studies in Jewish and Christian History*, vol. 1; Leiden: Brill, 1976: 167–200).

Birdsall, J. (1992) 'Introductory Survey', in *ABD* 6 'Versions, Ancient', 787–93.

Black, M., and W. Smalley (eds) (1974) *On Language, Culture, and Religion: In Honour of Eugene A. Nida* (The Hague, Paris: Mouton).

Bodine, Walter (1980) *The Greek Text of Judges* (Chicago, CA: Scholars Press).

Bogaert, P.M. (1985) 'Les etudes sur la Septante: Bilan et perspectives', *RTL* 16: 174–200.

— (1993) 'Septante et Versions Grecques', in J. Briend and E. Cothenet (eds), *Supplément au Dictionnaire de la Bible* (vol. 12; Paris: Letouzey and Ané), cols 538–692.

Bons, E., J. Joosten and S. Kessler (2002) *La Bible d'Alexandrie. 23.1. Les Douze Prophètes: Osée* (Paris: Editions du Cerf).

Borgen, P. (1984) 'Philo of Alexandria', in Stone 1984: 233–82.

— (1992) 'Philo of Alexandria', in *ABD* 5: 333–42.

— (1997) *Philo of Alexandria: An Exegete for his Time* (Leiden: Brill).

— (2000) *The Philo Index: A Complete Greek Word Index to the Writings of Philo of Alexandria* (Grand Rapids MI: Eerdmans; Leiden: Brill).

Boyd-Taylor, Cameron (1997) 'Esther's Great Adventure', *BIOSCS* 30: 81–113.

(1998) 'A Place in the Sun: The Interpretative Significance of LXX-Psalm 18:5c', *BIOSCS* 31: 71–105.

(2001) 'The Evidentiary Value of Septuagintal Usage for Greek Lexicography: Alice's Reply to Humpty Dumpty', *BIOSCS* 34: 47–80.

Brenner, Athalya, and Carole Fontaine (eds) (1997) *A Feminist Companion to Reading the Bible* (Sheffield: Sheffield Academic Press).

Brenton, Sir Lancelot (1851) *The Septuagint with Apocrypha: Greek and English* (London: Samuel Bagster & Sons; reprinted, Grand Rapids MI: Zondervan, 9th edn, 1982).

Brixhe, C. (ed.) (1993) *La Koiné Grecque Antique 1: une langue introuvable?* (Nancy: Presses Universitaires de Nancy).

Brock, Sebastian (1972) 'The Phenomenon of the Septuagint', *OTS* 17: 11–36.

Brock, S., C. Fritsch and S. Jellicoe (1973) *A Classified Bibliography of the Septuagint* (Leiden: Brill).

Brooke, A., N. McLean and H. St J. Thackeray (1906–40) *The Old Testament in Greek according to the Text of Codex Vaticanus* (Cambridge: Cambridge University Press).

Brooke, G., and B. Lindars (eds) (1992) *Septuagint, Scrolls and Cognate Writings* (Atlanta GA: SBL).

Brown, William P. (1999) 'Reassessing the Text-Critical Value of Septuagint-Genesis 1: A Response to Martin Rösel', *BIOSCS* 32: 35–9.

Büchner, Dirk (1997) 'On the Relationship between *Mekilta De Rabbi Ishmael* and Septuagint Exodus 12–23', in Taylor 1997: 403–20.

(2000) 'Translation Technique in the Septuagint Leviticus', in Porter 2000b: 92–106.

Burkitt, F. (1897) *Fragments of the Books of Kings According to the Translation of Aquila* (Cambridge: Cambridge University Press; reprinted New York, 1969), pp. xviii–xxii.

Charlesworth, James H. (ed.) (1983; 1985) *The Old Testament Pseudepigrapha* (2 vols; New York: Doubleday).

(2002) 'Biblical Stories and Quotations Reflected and Even Adumbrated in the Old Testament Pseudepigrapha', in Delamarter 2002: 1–6.

Coggins, Richard J. (1998) *Sirach* (Sheffield: Sheffield Academic Press).

Coggins, R., and L. Houlden (eds) (1990) *A Dictionary of Biblical Interpretation* (London: SCM Press).

Cohen, A. (ed.) (1965) *The Minor Tractates of the Talmud* (2 vols; London: Soncino Press).

Cohn, L., and P. Wendland (1896–1930) *Philonis Alexandrini Opera Quae Supersunt* (6 vols; Berlin: George Reimer).

Collins, Nina (1992) '281 BCE: the Year of the Translation of the Pentateuch into Greek under Ptolemy II', in Brooke and Lindars 1992: 403–503.

Colson, F. (1966) *Philo, with an English Translation* (LCL, vol. 6; London: Heinemann; Cambridge MA: Harvard University Press, 1935; reprinted 1966).

Colson, F., and G. Whitaker (1968) *Philo, with an English Translation* (LCL, vol. 5; London: Heinemann; Cambridge, MA: Harvard University Press, 1934; reprinted 1968).

Conybeare, F., and St George Stock (1905) *Selections from the Septuagint* (Boston, MA: Ginn; reprinted as *A Grammar of Septuagint Greek. With Selected Readings, Vocabularies and Updated Indexes*; Peabody MA: Hendrickson, 1995. A shorter version, without the reading passages, published by Grand Rapids MI: Zondervan, 1980).

Cook, Johann (1995) 'Were the Persons Responsible for the Septuagint Translators and/or Scribes and/or Editors?', *JNSL* 21: 45–58.

(1997) *The Septuagint of Proverbs: Jewish and/or Hellenistic Proverbs? Concerning the Hellenistic Colouring of Septuagint Proverbs* (VTSup 69; Leiden: Brill).

(2001) 'The Ideology of Septuagint Proverbs', in Taylor 2001: 463–79.

Cox, Claude E. (ed.) (1987) *VI Congress Volume of the IOSCS, 1986* (Atlanta GA: Scholars Press).

(1991) *VII Congress Volume of the IOSCS, 1989* (Atlanta GA: Scholars Press).

Craven, Toni (1983) *Artistry and Faith in the Book of Judith* (Chicago CA: Scholars Press).

Davies, W., and L. Finkelstein (eds) (1989) *The Cambridge History of Judaism* (vol. 2, *The Hellenistic Age*; Cambridge: Cambridge University Press).

Delamarter, Steve (2002) *A Scripture Index to Charlesworth's* The Old Testament Pseudepigrapha (Sheffield: Sheffield Academic Press).

Dimant, Devorah (1987) 'The Problem of Non-Translated Biblical Greek', in Cox 1987: 1–19.

Dines, Jennifer M. (1990) 'Septuagint', in Coggins and Houlden 1990: 622–5.

— (1992) 'The Septuagint of Amos: A Study in Interpretation'; University of London dissertation.

— (1995) 'Imaging Creation: The Septuagint Translation of Genesis 1:2', *HeyJ* 36: 439–50.

— (1998) 'Jerome and the Hexapla: The Witness of the *Commentary on Amos*', in Salvesen 1998: 421–36.

Dogniez, Cécile (1995) *A Bibliography of the Septuagint: 1970–1993* (VTSup 60; Leiden: Brill).

— (2001) 'La Bible d'Alexandrie II. Select Passage: Sophonie (Zephaniah) 3, 8–11', in Taylor 2001: 199–216.

Dogniez, C., and M. Harl (eds) (1992) *La Bible d'Alexandrie. 5. Le Deutéronome* (Paris: Editions du Cerf).

— (2001) *La Bible des Septante: Le Pentateuche d'Alexandrie* (Paris: Editions du Cerf).

Dorival, Gilles (1987) 'La Bible des Septante chez les auteurs païens (jusqu'au Pseudo-Longin)', in *Cahiers de Biblia Patristica* (Strasbourg: Centre d'Analyse et de Documentation Patristiques), pp. 9–26.

— (1999) 'Autour des titres des Psaumes', *Revue des sciences religieuses* 73: 165–76.

Dorival, G., and O. Munnich (eds) (1995) *Selon la Septante: Hommage à Marguerite Harl* (Paris: Editions du Cerf).

Epstein, I. (ed.) (1935–52) *The Babylonian Talmud* (London: Soncino Press).

Evans, Craig (1989) *To See and not Perceive: Isaiah 6:9–10 in Early Jewish and Christian Interpretation* (Sheffield: Sheffield Academic Press).

Evans, Trevor F. (2001) *Verbal Syntax in the Greek Pentateuch: Natural Greek Usage and Hebrew Interference* (Oxford: Oxford University Press).

Feldman, Martin (1988a) 'A Selective Critical Bibliography of Josephus', in Feldman and Hata 1988: 330–448.

(1988b) 'Josephus', in Mulder 1988: 455–518.

(1992) 'Josephus', in *ABD* 3: 981–98.

(1998) *Josephus' Interpretation of the Bible* (Berkeley CA, Los Angeles, London: University of California Press).

Feldman, M., and G. Hata (1988) *Josephus, the Bible and History* (Leiden: Brill).

Fernández Marcos, Natalio (1998) *Introducción a las Versiones griegas de la Biblia* (2nd edn revised and expanded; Madrid: Instituto de Filología del CSIC).

(2000) *The Septuagint in Context: Introduction to the Greek Versions of the Bible* (Brill: Leiden).

(2001) 'Reactions to the Panel on Modern Translations', in Taylor 2001: 235–40.

Field, Frederick (1875) *Origenis Hexaplorum Quae Supersunt* (Oxford: Oxford University Press).

Flint, P., and J. VanderKam (eds) (1998; 1999) *The Dead Sea Scrolls After Fifty Years: A Comprehensive Assessment* (2 vols; Leiden: Brill)

Fraser, P. (1972) *Ptolemaic Alexandria* (3 vols; Oxford: Clarendon Press).

Freedman, David Noel, *et al.* (eds) (1992) *The Anchor Bible Dictionary* (6 vols; New York: Doubleday).

Garbini, G. (1988) *History and Ideology in Ancient Israel* (London: SCM Press).

Gentry, Peter J. (1995) *The Asterisked Materials in the Greek Job* (Atlanta GA: Scholars Press).

(1998) 'The Place of Theodotion-Job in the Textual History of the Septuagint', in Salvesen 1998: 199–230.

Goldstein, Jonathan A. (1983) *2 Maccabees* (AB 41A; New York: Doubleday).

(1991) 'The Message of *Aristeas to Philocrates*. In the Second Century BCE, Obey the Torah, Venerate the Temple of Jerusalem, but Speak Greek, and put your Hopes in the Ptolemaic Dynasty', in Mor 1991: 1–23.

Gooding, D. (1976) *Relics of Ancient Exegesis: A Study in the Miscellanies in 3 Reigns 2* (Cambridge: Cambridge University Press).

Goodman, Martin (2001) 'Introduction to the Apocrypha', in Barton and Muddiman 2001: 617–26.

Grabbe, L. L. (1982) 'Aquila's Translation and Rabbinic Exegesis', *JJS* 33: 527–36.

   (1992a) *Judaism from Cyrus to Hadrian. I. Persian and Greek Periods. II. Roman Period* (Minneapolis MN: Fortress Press; one-vol. edn, London: SCM Press, 1994).

   (1992b) 'The Translation Technique of the Greek Minor Versions: Translations or Revisions?', in Brooke and Lindars 1992: 505–56.

Grant, Robert (1970) *Theophilus of Antioch*, Ad Autolycum: Text and Translation (Oxford: Clarendon Press).

Greenspoon, Leonard J. (1987) 'The Use and Abuse of the Term "LXX" and Related Terminology in Recent Scholarship', *BIOSCS* 20: 21–9.

   (1990) 'Recensions, Revisions, Rabbinics: D. Barthélemy and Early Developments in the Greek Traditions', *Textus* 15: 153–67.

   (1992a) 'Greek Versions', in *ABD* 6: 793–4.

   (1992b) 'Theodotion's Version', in *ABD* 6: 447–8.

   (1992c) 'Aquila's Version', in *ABD* 1: 320–1.

   (1992d) 'Symmachus' Version', in *ABD* 6: 251.

   (1998) 'The Dead Sea Scrolls and the Greek Bible', in Flint and VanderKam 1998: 101–27.

Griffiths, J. (1987) 'Egypt and the Rise of the Synagogue', *JTS* 38: 1–15.

Grube, G. M. A. (1991) *Longinus* 'On Great Writing' ('On the Sublime') (Indianopolis/Cambridge: Hackett Publishing Company, 1st printed 1957).

Gruen, Erich (1998) *Heritage and Hellenism: The Reinvention of Jewish Tradition* (Berkeley CA, Los Angeles, London: University of California Press).

Hadas, M. (1951) *Aristeas to Philocrates (Letter of Aristeas)* (New York: Harper).

Harl, Marguerite (1986) *La Bible d'Alexandrie. 1. La Genèse* (Paris: Editions du Cerf).

(1988) 'On the Septuagint', *BJGS* 3: 15–18.

(1992) *La Langue de Japhet: Quinze Etudes sur la Septante et le Grec des Chrétiens* (Paris: Editions du Cerf).

(1993) '*La Bible d'Alexandrie* et les Etudes sur la Septante', *VC* 47: 313–40.

(1998) 'Translating the Septuagint: Experience of "La Bible d'Alexandrie"', *BIOSCS* 31: 31–5.

(1999) 'L'Usage des Commentaires Patristiques pour l'Etude de la Septante', *Revue des sciences religieuses* 73: 184–201.

(2001) 'La Bible d'Alexandrie. 1. The Translation Principles', in Taylor 2001: 181–97.

Harl, M., G. Dorival and O. Munnich (1988) *La Bible Grecque des Septante: Du Judaisme Hellénistique au Christianisme Ancien* (Paris: Editions du Cerf; 2nd edn, Paris: Editions du Cerf, CNRS, 1994).

Harlé, P., and D. Pralon (1988) *La Bible d'Alexandrie. 3. Le Lévitique* (Paris: Editions du Cerf).

Hatch, E., and H. Redpath (1897–1906) *A Concordance to the Septuagint and the other Greek Versions of the Old Testament, including the Apocryphal Books* (3 vols; Oxford: Clarendon Press; reprinted in one volume, with new introductory material, by E. Tov and R. Kraft, and with T. Muraoka's *Hebrew-Aramaic Index*, by Grand Rapids MI: Baker Books, 1998).

Hayes, John (ed.) (1999) *The Dictionary of Biblical Interpretation* (Nashville TN: Abingdon Press).

Hegermann, Harald (1989) 'The Diaspora in the Hellenistic Age', in Davies and Finkelstein 1989: 115–66.

Hiebert, Robert (2000) 'Translation Technique in LXX Genesis and its Implications for the NETS Version', *BIOSCS* 33: 76–93.

(2001) 'Translating a translation: The Septuagint of Genesis and the NETS Project', in Taylor 2001: 263–84.

Holladay, C. (1983) *Fragments from Hellenistic Jewish Authors, Volume 1, Historians* (Chico CA: Scholars Press).

(1992) 'Aristobulus (OT Pseudepigrapha)', in *ABD* 1: 383–4.

(1995) *Fragments from Hellenistic Jewish Authors, Volume 3, Aristobulus* (Chico CA: University of California Press).

Holmes, R., and J. Parsons (1798–1827) *Vetus Testamentum Graecum cum variis lectionibus* (Oxford: Clarendon Press).

Horbury, William (1988) 'OT Interpretation in the Writings of the Church Fathers', in Mulder 1988: 727–87.

(2001) 'The Wisdom of Solomon', in Barton and Muddiman 2001: 650–67.

Horrocks, Geoffrey (1997) *Greek: A History of the Language and its Speakers* (London: Longman).

Horsley, G. (1989) 'The Fiction of "Jewish Greek"', in G. Horsley (ed.), *New Documents Illustrating Early Christianity* (Sydney: McQuarie University), pp. 5–40.

van der Horst, P. (1988) 'The Interpretation of the Bible by the Minor Hellenistic Jewish Authors', in Mulder 1988: 519–46.

Howard, G. (1974) 'The Quinta of the Minor Prophets', *Biblica* 55: 15–22.

Isaacs, Marie E. (1976) *The Concept of Spirit : A Study of Pneuma in Hellenistic Judaism and its Bearing on the New Testament* (London: Heythrop College).

Jarick, John (1990) 'Aquila's Koheleth', *Textus* 15: 131–9.

Jellicoe, Sidney (1968) *The Septuagint and Modern Study* (Oxford: Clarendon Press).

Jenkins, R. G. (1998a) 'Hexaplaric Marginalia and the Hexapla-Tetrapla Question', in Salvesen 1998: 73–87.

(1998b) 'The First Column of the Hexapla: The Evidence of the Milan Codex (Rahlfs 1098) and the Cairo Genizah Fragment (Rahlfs 2005)', in Salvesen 1998: 88–102.

Jobes, Karen H., and Moisés Silva (2000) *Invitation to the Septuagint* (Grand Rapids MI: Baker Academic).

Johnson, L. T. (1986) *The Writings of the New Testament: An Interpretation* (London: SCM Press).

Joosten, Jan (2000) 'Une Théologie de la Septante? Réflexions méthodologiques sur l'interprétation de la version grecque', *RTP* 132: 31–46.

Kamesar, Adam (1993) *Jerome, Greek Scholarship, and the Hebrew Bible: A Study of the* Quaestiones Hebraicae in Genesim (Oxford: Clarendon Press).

168 *The Septuagint*

(2002) 'Writing Commentaries on the Works of Philo: Some Reflexions', *Adamantius* 8: 127–34.

Kasher, A. (1991) 'Political and National Connections between the Jews of Ptolemaic Egypt and their Brethren in Eretz Israel', in Mor 1991: 224–41.

Kelly, J. (1975) *Jerome: His Life, Writings, and Controversies* (London: Duckworth).

Kenyon, F. (1975) *The Text of the Greek Bible* (London: Duckworth, 1936; 3rd edn, revised by A. Adams, 1975).

Klein, R. (1974) *Textual Criticism of the Old Testament: The Septuagint after Qumran* (Philadelphia PA: Fortress Press).

Knobloch, F. (1998) 'Web Review: The Perseus Digital Library', *BIOSCS* 31: 49–61.

(2000) 'Web Review: The Christian Classics Ethereal Library, et al', *BIOSCS* 33: 36–8.

van der Kooij, Arie (2001) 'Comments on NETS and *La Bible d'Alexandrie*', in Taylor 2001: 229–31.

Kreuzer, Siegfried (2001) 'A German Translation of the Septuagint', *BIOSCS* 34: 40–5.

de Lange, Nicholas (1976) *Origen and the Jews: Studies in Jewish-Christian Relations in Third-century Palestine* (Cambridge: Cambridge University Press).

Lee, J. A. L. (1983) *A Lexical Study of the Septuagint Version of the Pentateuch* (Chico CA: Scholars Press).

(1997) 'Translations of the Old Testament. 1. Greek', in Porter 1997: 775–83.

(2003) '*A Lexical Study* Thirty Years on, with Observations on "Order" Words in the LXX Pentateuch', in Shalom M. Paul *et al.* (eds), *Emanuel: Studies in Hebrew Bible Septuagint and Dead Sea Scrolls in Honour of Emanuel Tov* (Leiden, Boston: Brill).

Leisegang, J. (1926) Index Volume to Cohn and Wendland 1896–1930 (vol. 7; Berlin: W. de Gruyter).

Leonas, A. (1999) 'The Septuagint and the Magical Papyri: Some Preliminary Notes', *BIOSCS* 32: 51–64.

(2001) 'Patristic Evidence of Difficulties in Understanding the LXX: Hadrian's Philological Remarks in *Isagoge*', in Taylor 2001: 393–414.

Longenecker, R. (1975) *Biblical Exegesis in the Apostolic Period* (Grand Rapids MI: Eerdmans).

Lust, J., E. Eynikel and K. Hauspie (1992) *A Greek-English Lexicon of the Septuagint* (2 vols; Stuttgart: Deutsche Bibelgesellschaft; revised edn, 1 vol., 2003).

McLay, R. Timothy (1998) 'The Theodotion and Old Greek Texts of Daniel', in Salvesen 1998: 231–54.

—— (1999) 'Web Review: The CATSS Data Base', *BIOSCS* 32: 44–6.

—— (2003) *The Use of the Septuagint in New Testament Research* (Grand Rapids MI, Cambridge UK: Eerdmans).

Marcus, R. (1933) *Josephus, with an English Translation. Vol. 7, Jewish Antiquities, Books 12–14* (LCL; 9 vols; Cambridge MA: Harvard University Press; London: Heinemann).

Meecham, Henry (1935) *The Letter of Aristeas: A Linguistic Study with Special Reference to the Greek Bible* (Manchester: Manchester University Press).

Metzger, Bruce (1977) *The Early Versions of the New Testament: Their Origin, Transmission and Limitation* (Oxford: Oxford University Press).

—— (1981) *Manuscripts of the Greek Bible: An Introduction to Palaeography* (New York, Oxford: Oxford University Press).

Mor, M. (ed.) (1991) *Eretz Israel, Israel and the Jewish Diaspora. Mutual Relations* (Lanham MA, New York, London: University Press of America).

Mulder, M. (1988) *Mikra: Text, Translation, Reading and Interpretation of the Hebrew Bible in Ancient Judaism and Early Christianity* (Assen, Maastricht: Van Gorcum; Philadelphia PA: Fortress Press).

Müller, Mogens (1996) *The First Bible of the Church: A Plea for the Septuagint* (Sheffield: Sheffield Academic Press).

Munnich, Olivier (1987) 'Contribution à l'étude de la première révision de la Septante', *ANRW* 20: 190–220.

Muraoka, Takamitsu (1973) 'Literary Device in the Septuagint', *Textus* 8: 20–30.

—— (1998) *A Hebrew-Aramaic Index to the Septuagint (Keyed to the Hatch-Redpath Concordance)* (Grand Rapids MI: Baker Books).

(2002a) *A Greek-English Lexicon of the Septuagint: Chiefly of the Pentateuch and the Twelve Prophets* (Louvain, Paris, Dudley MA: Peeters).

(2002b) 'Introduction Générale aux Douze Prophètes', in Bons, Joosten and Kessler 2002: i–xxiii.

Murray, Oswyn (1967) 'Aristeas and Ptolemaic Kingship', *JTS* 18: 337–71.

Norton, Gerard J. (1997) 'Collecting Data for a new edition of the Fragments of the Hexapla', in Taylor 1997: 251–62.

(1998) 'Observations on the First Two Columns of the Hexapla', in Salvesen 1998: 103–24.

O'Fearghail, F. (1989) 'The Imitation of the Septuagint in Luke's Infancy Narrative', *PIBA* 12: 58–78.

Olofsson, Staffan (1990) *God is my Rock: A Study of Translation Technique and Theological Exegesis in the Septuagint* (Stockholm: Almqvist and Wiksell).

(1997) 'The *Kaige* Group and the Septuagint Book of Psalms', in Taylor 1997: 189–230.

Orlinsky, H. (1975) 'The Septuagint as Holy Writ and the Philosophy of the Translators', *HUCA* 46: 89–114.

(1989) 'The Septuagint and its Hebrew Text', in Davies and Finkelstein 1989: 534–62.

Otzen, Benedikt (2002) *Tobit and Judith* (London, New York: Sheffield Academic Press).

Parker, D. (1992) 'Hexapla of Origen, The', in *ABD* 3: 188–9.

Parsons, Peter (1990) 'The Scripts and their Date', in Tov 1990: 19–26.

Pelletier, A. (1962) *Lettre d'Aristée à Philocrate* (SC 89; Paris: Editions du Cerf).

(1988) 'Josephus, the Letter of Aristeas, and the Septuagint', in Feldman and Hata 1988: 97–115.

Peters, M. (1992) 'Septuagint', in *ABD* 5: 1093–1104.

Pietersma, A. (1985) 'Septuagint Research: A Plea for a Return to Basic Issues', *VT* 35: 296–311.

(1996) *Translation Manual for "A New English Translation of the Septuagint (NETS)"* (Ada MI: Uncial Books).

(2000a) *A New English Translation of the Septuagint: The Psalms* (New York, Oxford: Oxford University Press).

(2000b) 'The Present State of the Critical Text of the Greek Psalter', in Aejmelaeus and Quast 2000: 12–32.

(2001a) 'Exegesis and Liturgy in the Superscriptions of the Greek Psalter', in Taylor 2001: 99–138.

(2001b) 'A New English Translation of the Septuagint', in Taylor 2001: 217–28.

Pietersma, A., and B. Wright (eds) (1998) 'A Prospectus for a Commentary on the Septuagint, sponsored by the IOSCS', *BIOSCS* 31: 43–8.

Porter, Stanley (2000a) 'The Functional Distribution of Koine Greek in First-Century Palestine', in Porter 2000b: 53–78.

Porter, S. (ed.) (1997) *Handbook of Classical Rhetoric in the Hellenistic Period, 330 BC – AD 400* (Leiden: Brill).

(2000b) *Diglossia and Other Topics in New Testament Linguistics* (Sheffield: Sheffield Academic Press).

Rahlfs, Alfred (1914) *Verzeichnis der griechischen Handshriften des Altens Testaments* (MSU 2; Göttingen: Vandenhoeck and Ruprecht, 1914; Berlin: Weidmannsche Buchhandlung, 1915).

(1935) *Septuaginta. Id est Vetus Testamentum graece iuxta LXX interpretes* (2 vols; Stuttgart: Deutsche Bibelgesellschaft; one-vol. edn, 1979).

Rajak, Tessa (1983) *Josephus: The Historian and his Society* (London: Duckworth; 2nd edn. 2002).

Reif, Stefan (1993) *Judaism and Hebrew Prayer* (Cambridge: Cambridge University Press).

Reinhartz, Adele (2001) 'Esther (Greek)', in Barton and Muddiman 2001: 642–9.

Rengstorf, K. (1973–83) *A Complete Concordance to Flavius Josephus* (4 vols; Leiden: Brill).

Roberts, C. (1936) *Two Biblical Papyri in the John Rylands Library Manchester* (Manchester: Manchester University Press, and the Librarian, The John Rylands Library).

(1970) 'Books in the Ancient World', in Ackroyd and Evans 1970: 30–66.

Rösel, Martin (1994) *Übersetzung als Vollendung der Auslegung: Studien zur Genesis-Septuaginta* (*BZAW* 223; Berlin, New York: W. de Gruyter).

(1998) 'The Text-Critical Value of Septuagint-Genesis', *BIOSCS* 31: 62–70.

Salvesen, Alison (1991) *Symmachus in the Pentateuch* (Manchester: University of Manchester, Journal of Semitic Studies).

Salvesen, Alison (ed.) (1998) *Origen's Hexapla and Fragments* (Tübingen: Mohr Siebeck).

Schaper, Joachim (1995) *Eschatology in the Greek Psalter* (Tübingen: Mohr Siebeck).

(1998) 'The Origin and Purpose of the Fifth Column of the Hexapla', in Salvesen 1998: 3–15.

Schürer, E. (1986) *The History of the Jewish People in the Time of Christ* (vol. 3.i; revised and edited by G. Vermes *et al.*, Edinburgh: T. & T. Clark).

Seeligmann, I. L. (1948) *The Septuagint Version of Isaiah: A Discussion of its Problems* (Leiden: Brill).

Shutt, R. (1985) 'Letter of Aristeas (Third Century BC – First Century AD). A New Translation and Introduction', in Charlesworth 1985: 7–34.

(1992) 'Aristeas, Letter of', in *ABD* 1: 380–2.

Simonetti, Manlio (1994) *Biblical Interpretation in the Early Church: An Historical Introduction to Patristic Exegesis* (Edinburgh: T. & T. Clark).

Siquans, Agnethe (2002) *Der Deuteronomium-kommentar des Theodoret von Kyros* (Frankfurt am Main, Oxford, Wien: Peter Lang).

Skeat, T. (1999) 'The Codex Sinaiticus, the Codex Vaticanus and Constantine', *JTS* 50: 583–625.

Soderlund, Sven (1985) *The Greek Text of Jeremiah: A Revised Hypothesis* (Sheffield: *JSOT* Press).

Sollamo, R. (2001) 'The Letter of Aristeas and the Origin of the Septuagint', in Taylor 2001: 329–42.

Spottorno, Mª Victoria (1997) 'The Books of Chronicles in Josephus' *Jewish Antiquities*', in Taylor 1997: 381–90.

Stone, Michael (ed.) (1984) *Jewish Writings of the Second Temple Period* (Assen: Van Gorcum).

Swete, H. B. (1887–94) *The Old Testament in Greek* (3 vols; Cambridge: Cambridge University Press).

(1914) *An Introduction to the Old Testament in Greek* (Cambridge: Cambridge University Press, 1900; revised by R. R. Ottley, 1914; reprinted Peabody MA: Hendrickson, 1989).

Taylor, Bernard A. (1994) *The Analytical Lexicon to the Septuagint: A Complete Parsing Guide* (Grand Rapids MI: Zondervan).

Taylor, Bernard A. (ed.) (1997) *IX Congress Volume of the IOSCS, 1995* (Chico CA: Scholars Press).

(2001) *X Congress Volume of the IOSCS, 1998* (Chico CA: *SBL*).

Taylor, C. (1900) *Hebrew-Greek Genizah Palimpsests* (Cambridge: Cambridge University Press).

Thackeray, Henry St John (1909) *A Grammar of the Old Testament in Greek according to the Septuagint* (vol. 1; Cambridge: Cambridge University Press).

(1917) *The Letter of Aristeas* (London: SPCK).

(1923) *The Septuagint and Jewish Worship: A Study in Origins* (The Schweich Lectures, 1920; 2nd edn, London: Oxford University Press).

Tov, Emanuel (1976) *The Septuagint Translation of Jeremiah and Baruch – A Discussion of an Early Revision of Jeremiah 29–52 and Baruch 1:1–3:8* (Missoula MT: Harvard University Press).

(1984) 'The Rabbinic Tradition about the "Alterations" Inserted into the Greek Pentateuch and their Relation to the Original Text of the LXX', *JSJ* 15: 65–89.

(1987) 'The Nature and Study of the Translation Technique of the Septuagint in the Past and Present', in Cox 1987: 337–59.

(1988) 'The Septuagint', in Mulder 1988: 161–88.

(1990) *The Greek Minor Prophets Scroll from Naḥal Ḥever (8ḤevXIIgr)* (DJD 8; Oxford: Oxford University Press).

(1997) *The Text Critical Use of the Septuagint in Biblical Research* (revised and enlarged 2nd edn; Jerusalem: Simor).

(1999) *The Greek and Hebrew Bible: Collected Essays on the Septuagint* (Leiden: Brill).

Tov, Emanuel, and Benjamin Wright (1985) 'Computer-Assisted Study of the Criteria for Assessing the Literalness of Translation Units in the Septuagint', *Textus* 12: 151–87.

de Troyer, Kristin (1997) 'Septuagint and Gender Studies: The Very Beginning of a Promising Liaison', in Brenner and Fontaine 1997: 326–43.

Ulrich, Eugene (2000) 'The Dead Sea Scrolls and their Implications for an Edition of the Septuagint Psalter', in Aejmelaeus and Quast 2000: 323–65.

Veltri, G. (1994) *Eine Tora für den König Talmai* (Tübingen: Mohr Siebeck).

Voitila, Anssi (1997) 'The Translator of the Greek Numbers', in Taylor 1997: 109–21.

Wade, Martha (2000) 'Evaluating Lexical Consistency in the Old Greek Bible', *BIOSCS* 33: 53–75.

— (2003) *Consistency of Translation Techniques in the Tabernacle Accounts of Exodus in the Old Greek* (Atlanta GA: Society of Biblical Literature).

Walter, N. (1964) *Der Thoraausleger Aristobulus* (TU 86; Berlin: Akademie-Verlag).

— (1989) 'Jewish-Greek Literature of the Greek Period', in Davies and Finkelstein 1989: 385–408.

Wevers, J. W. (1988) 'Barthélemy and Proto-Septuagint Studies', *BIOSCS* 21: 23–34.

— (1991) 'The Göttingen Pentateuch: Some Post-Partem [*sic*] Reflections', in Cox 1991: 51–60.

— (1993) *Notes on the Greek Text of Genesis* (Atlanta GA: Scholars Press).

— (1997) 'The LXX Translator of Deuteronomy', in Taylor 1997: 57–89.

— (1999) 'Septuagint', in *DBI*, pp. 457–62.

Wiles, M. (1970) 'Origen as a Biblical Scholar', in Ackroyd and Evans 1970: 454–89.

Williams, Margaret (1998) *The Jews Among the Greeks and Romans: A Diaspora Sourcebook* (London: Duckworth).

Williamson, R. (1989) *Jews in the Hellenistic World. 1.2. Philo* (Cambridge: Cambridge University Press).

Wills, L. (trans. and ed.) (2002) *Ancient Jewish Novels: An Anthology* (Oxford: Oxford University Press).

Winston, D. (1996) 'Aristobulus: from Walter to Holladay', *Studia Philonica Annual* 8: 155–66.

(1999) 'Aristobulus of Paneas', in *DBI*, pp. 56–7.

Wolff, H. W. (1977) *Joel and Amos: A Commentary on the Books of the Prophets Joel and Amos* (Hermeneia; Philadelphia PA: Fortress Press).

Wright, Benjamin (1987) 'The Quantitative Representation of Elements: Evaluating "Literalism" in the Septuagint', in Cox 1987: 310–35.

Würthwein, E. (1980) *The Text of the Old Testament: An Introduction to the* Biblia Hebraica (London: SCM Press), Chapter 5.

Yadin, Y., *et al.* (eds) (2002) *The Documents from the Bar Kokhba Period in the Cave of Letters: Hebrew, Aramaic and Nabataean-Aramaic Papyri* (Jerusalem: Israel Exploration Society).

Yarbro Collins, A. (1985) 'Aristobulus', in Charlesworth 1985: 831–42.

Ziegler, Joseph (1939) *Isaias* (Septuaginta, vol. 14; Göttingen: Vandenhoeck and Ruprecht).

(1943) *Duodecim Prophetae* (Septuaginta, vol. 13; Göttingen: Vandenhoeck and Ruprecht).

(1965) *Sapientia Iesu Filii Sirach* (Septuaginta, vol. 12.2; Göttingen: Vandenhoeck and Ruprecht).

INDEXES

Index of References

Books of the Septuagint (following the order in Rahlfs)

Dead Sea Scrolls

Papyri (Jewish and Christian)

Hellenistic Jewish Sources

Classical Sources

Index of Authors

183

General Index

187